How to Get Laid in Less Than Three Dates

How to Get Laid in Less Than Three Dates

By TayloR Puck, M.S., M.Ed.

Edited by Kelly M. Apgar

Acknowledgments:

I'd like to thank the following people for encouraging me to write this book, and adding their two, three or four cents: Frank, Molly D'Alessio, Tray, Kev, Allison Miller, Jen, Dawn, Dean, Mike Citarella, Palmer, Giovanni Gianni, Ed & Claudia, Kim & Ron, MJ, Steven, Jeremiah Lindsey, Ryan "horse cock" Quigley, Brett Justin, Margaret Morris, Scott Thomas, Christopher Sapanaro & Kristin Leone, Emily Gatto, Rash Behavior, Tangie, Ray Donato, Kimberly Girlock, Tina, Mark SanGiacomo, Mike Forte, Scott Redding, Lindsey S. Nagy, Kate, Shannon Lynn Grace, Jessie, Colin Hall, Jeff Disko, Pat Van Deusen, Bob B., and the notorious threesome: Jack, Hockey and Kona.

A special appreciation to my family for not disowning me...

And a final thank you to my personal editor, Kelly M. Apgar.

This book has been written in memory of my Love, C~. Without your love, support and impetuous advocacy, I would have never found the determination to follow through with this project. Thank you!

Introduction

This book is intended for men who are trying to bang a dime without wasting time. This is not your average dating guide. With these instructions, you'll be able to fuck your dream girl! But, if you are satisfied with having one night stands with the pretty secretary who giggles at your jokes and watches you from afar – good for you! On the other hand, if you are tired of the annoying, insecure little girl who you direct towards the Rejection Hotline after a one night roll in the hay, then continue reading.

Throughout this book, you will utilize helpful hints from a *woman's* perspective, and become skilled at understanding how confident, independent women perceive men. In the end, you will look forward to sampling your new commentary and facing the challenge of attracting a woman you would be proud to be with.

This book will serve as a stereotypical, but true "how to" for men who are looking to upgrade the clientele on their fuck list. If you are looking to knock some boots with a confident, beautiful woman, you need to understand what we are looking for. A confident woman is self-assured in the bedroom. We know we're damn sexy! In return, we expect a man who knows what he is doing. If you show us any sign of doubt, we will lose interest immediately.

The truth is women will have no problem giving it up if you have the possible potential of being "the one". After the age of 25, most women are sexually experienced, and if this holds true for your prospective lay, her sex drive should be equal to, if not stronger, than yours. A woman who is searching for a partner is looking for a sexual union. She'll know if she has that connection with you within the first five minutes of meeting you. If she is interested in you, this longing for sexual gratification will be obvious. The secret that this book is trying to elucidate is even if she doesn't feel the connection, *there's still a chance she'll sleep with you*!

At this moment you might be thinking, "I'm not looking for anything serious. I just want to fuck a hot girl!" Men, my goal as your guide is to get you laid by the third date. Whatever your prerogative is thereafter is none of my concern. You want to marry the girl? Never call her again? Great! Once you get laid my job is done, so lets get down to business!

Topics

The Oedipus Complex

She Works **Hard** for the Money

So **Hard** for it Honey

Bitch vs. Dick

Meerkats

Checklist

Wipe the Glass

It's Not a Lie...If You Believe It

FishingWithDynamite.com

Joygasm

Dutch People Are Ugly

The Robber or the Robbee

Game Off

Fucking Like Rabbits

Flooding the Basement

Netjobbing

You, Yourself & Yours

Your New Haircut

Fine Wine

Condom Sense

The Other Woman

Aspiration? More like Masturbatation!

Junk in *Your* Trunk

Gaspirilla

100-300 Yards

Circle Jerk

Ghettoization

Sexting

Velcro

East Coast vs. West Side

Your Fish Seems Confused!

Obama or Osama?

Jammin'

Fumble

Noodling

Deep as a Puddle

I Work Out!

Zumanity

Smart-Ass

Woman's Best Friend

Whiskey Dick

Around the World-And Back Again

Just Kidding!

Vote for Summer

My Eyes Are Up Here!

Let's Talk About Sex I

The Oedipus Complex

What you shouldn't say:

"My mom decorated my apartment."

"You remind me of my mom."

What you should say:

"My parents live in (pick a state *other* than the one you live in)."

"I talk to my parents once a week."

It's not that we necessarily *believe* in this concept, but it is a theory, that for some reason, our high schools have drilled into our heads four years of our lives while studying Shakespeare. Again, we don't necessarily assume that you are sexually attracted to your mother but we are aware of the unspoken bond between you and your mom. At least, we hope it's unspoken...

Isn't it strange how you spent nine months trying to get out of a woman and spend the rest of your life trying to get back in one? So do we...so take a clue, and cut the ties. Those of us who have been in a serious relationship know the mother eventually becomes an inconvenience. And for those of us who have never experienced horror stories of the boyfriend's mother, we have heard the terrifying tales of the mother-in-law. Whether she is over-bearing, annoying, nosey or just plain needy, we don't want any part of it. We know in the end, she will always be judging us. And at this point in our relationship, we are not interested in hearing stories about how important of a role model she is in your life.

It is good to refer to 'your parents' as a whole, instead of distinguishing the difference between your mother and father. Unless your parents are divorced, do your best to keep them as 'one'. It's acceptable if you mention, "My Dad and I love to fish." It's even alright to say a general statement like, "My Mom is a freak when it comes to Christmas decorations." But each sentence you make regarding your Mom is one strike against you.

Why, you ask? Other than the fact that *we* want to be the only woman in our man's life, consider the following scenario: You mention your mother loves to

13

watch *ABC's Desperate Housewives*-so do we. You say, "My mother hates cooking, but loves to bake cookies." We think, "So do I!" You explain how you, your father and your brother always want to spend your family vacations in Colorado so you can ski in the fresh snow, but your mother somehow always wins the fight. She enjoys lounging on a tropical beach surrounded by water and Pina Coladas. At this point, our eyes widen and our stomach churns in disgust. The last thing we want is to remind you of your mother. When was the last time you had sex with a girl that reminded you of your mom? Hopefully NEVER! But if we are getting the idea that you are looking for a motherly girlfriend-we are out of there!

Get it straight, boys!! We have our lives together. We are respectable women! We are not looking for a relationship where we have to tell you to get up early, clean your room, brush your teeth, or take the garbage out! We need a man who already has a semi-organized life, otherwise, once we start reminding you to do your chores, you'll describe us as "nagging". We have our own lives to worry about. If we want children, we'll ask you to help us. We don't want you to be one.

It's not that we don't want your mother to be a part of your life. We are just hoping that she once played a significant part, and didn't suffer too much when you fled the nest. Staying in touch with your parents on a regular basis is good. It shows your family is functional and knowing that draws us to you.

Beware Jewish boys and only children! Unfortunately, you already have two strikes against you. Most of the worst mother-son stories depict you. Jewish women have a reputation! They are overly critical of their sons' new love interest, ESPECIALLY if we're not Jewish! As for only children, if your mother's life revolves around your achievements and she still treats you like you were ten, you're in trouble. The best bet is to *never* mention your mother. Once again, discussing your parents is fine, but don't comment specifically on your mom. It sucks, we know. But girls talk and it seems as though the two of these categories appear to have the most protective, nosey and obnoxious mothers. To put it simply, we're not interested.

If you think this topic isn't true, and you consider the Oedipus complex as the biggest load of bullshit you've ever heard of, don't try to convince us. She was the first woman who ever let you suck on her tits, and don't try to tell us there's nothing sexual about that! If you want a woman who resembles your mother, go cougar hunting somewhere else!

She Works *Hard* for the Money

What you shouldn't say:

"Who'd you blow for that job?"

"Do you always dress that way for work?"

What you should say:

"So, tell me about your job."

"You seem very passionate about your work! That's awesome! And rare."

Some of us were raised by parents who lived in a fantasy world. They gave us strict instructions to ensure our happiness. "You'll graduate high school and go to college, where you'll meet your husband. After you get your degree, you'll get married, buy a house and start a family." Well, for those of us who had liars as parents, we had to make a choice! Most of us decided to further our career, the others became lesbians.

Sure, we want to be able to buy the latest styles. And yes! We want to appear strong and independent. But the real reason why successful women engulf themselves into a career is because we have nothing else to do! Honestly, if we were knocked up by the football captain at the age of 19, we wouldn't be where we are today. In fact, if we had fallen in love with the Keg Stand King at a fraternity party during sophomore year we'd probably be playing house. But since Mr. Right has still not made his appearance, we decided to better ourselves in another way. So we gave thanks to the Women's Movement and began our attempts to conquer the business world. If Rosie can do it, why can't we?

Something happens to a woman who decides to climb up on the ladder. Like the male tycoon, she tastes power and likes it. Her career becomes more than a hobby and she dives in head first. But just because she becomes more focused on her job doesn't make her lose sight of her original goals. Sure, she might have her own little black book filled with beneficial friends in different zip codes, but that still does not defeat the fact that she wants to get married and have that house filled with kids. Over time, she doesn't want different things-she wants *it all*!

Here's another thing to know about successful women. **We don't settle.** This is not good news for you, but if you make the cut-you must be one hell of a catch! As we age, we become thankful for not settling down at an early age. While we're in our late twenties/early thirties still enjoying happy hour after work, our college roommates are yelling over the screams of their crying babies. The first round of divorces starts, even though you spent over a thousand dollars the year before being a part of their wedded bliss. It turns out the younger you make a decision, the better the chance you'll regret it later in life. Meanwhile, while all of our friends are drowning in marital drama, we're on top of our game, playing by our own rules and enjoying every minute. We just hope we can find someone sooner or later to share it with.

This may be a lot for you to wrap your head around, and for some of you, you'll never fully comprehend a woman's desire. You just need to see the difference between a successful woman and a waste of space. Let's take a look at the Upper East Side between the hours of 1-3pm. Here you'll find the ladies who just finished having lunch with a friend. They'll be drunk from having 4 margaritas before noon. But no worries! They'll sober up by shopping until rush hour, while holding their $2,000 *Louie Vuitton* bag, wearing their $10,000 *Cartier* earrings, $2,800 *Monolo Blahniks* and $720 *Hermes* pasmina-and those are just her accessories! Late at night, they'll be drinking their bottle of wine while waiting for their husbands to come home. These are the women who have no purpose…waiting….driving themselves crazy, wondering whether or not her husband is fucking his secretary. The next day, her psychologist convinces her to drown her sorrows in inventive ways such as practicing yoga or participating in a fundraiser. (Basically, getting out of the house and spending more of their husband's money.) Is the distinction clear yet?

Yes, we are happy with ourselves and the decisions we've made even if we're going stag to our family's reunion. If there's one thing you should walk away with after reading this book it's we're not looking to settle. If we feel as though we can do better, we will. And you'll go down quicker than an Irish Car Bomb. The woman you're with wants it all. So *give* it to her!

So *Hard* for it Honey

What you shouldn't say:

When your phone rings and you check to see who's calling, "Don't you just hate collection agencies? They're *sooo* annoying."

"I work 24/7."

What you should say:

"I love my job."

"I've worked there for (and name an extended amount of time over two years)."

Because of the media exposing the following relationships: Hugh Heffner and Kimberly Conrad, Donald Trump and Melania Knauss, Mel Gibson and the Jew-I mean the Russian floozie, etc., it has been drilled into your heads that young, beautiful women look for men with money. This may reign true for the woman who doesn't have the brains to support the lifestyle she wants to live, but wake up boys! We are no longer MAD women from the 1950's! Lots of women pursue their education, attend college and have their own career. While your salary may be a bonus, it probably won't make or break a deal.

The women this book is helping you try to attract take offense when they hear comments insinuating that women use men for money. Financially speaking, these women are not looking for a sugar-daddy. They are searching for some sort of match. A healthy competition! Someone who is not only afraid to admit their woman can hold their own, but who's proud of it. Secretly, we want you to feel as though you have the financial power. We prefer it this way because it adds to your masculinity, which you will find in later chapters, that we are sexually attracted to.

What most women are looking for is a man who A) has a job, B) loves his job, and C) makes equal to or more than we do. Can a relationship work with two out of three? Perhaps, but it would require a lot of work. Let me explain:

Don't ever tell a girl you're in between jobs. It causes anxiety, and though this may sound completely asinine, the real reason why we fear this statement is because we care what other people think. If we tell a friend, "I spent three hours of my life last night which I will never get back. My date maxed out his credit card when he tried to buy me a piece of pizza. It turns out he's occupationally challenged," it's ok because we are sensible enough not to waste our time with an unemployed loser. On the other hand, if we choose to date you, telling our mother, "The economy is really bad right now," makes us feel like shit. She knows we can do better, and the truth is we do too.

Even if you can get her to accept your joblessness, it will eventually have a negative effect. The lack of money, blob-like laziness or your excessive free time will ultimately strain your relationship. You're bound to eventually catch the Hawaiian disease Laconookie.

You must enjoy what you do! If not, we will be concerned. We don't want to hear you bitch about your work every day and every night you come home. That's our time and we don't want you to be the type that brings the work drama home. We want a man who can separate their personal and work life. We also want a guy who has a meaningful career. If you're the type of guy that describes his job as one that "pays the bills", it's not a turn on. Why is your love for your work a concern for us? Isn't it obvious? We want a happy man! It makes us happy in return. Your career is a huge chunk of your life and it you're not happy with it, we'll have to deal with the exhausted, pissed off zombie that comes home weeknights-that is if you don't become an alcoholic from getting blitzed at happy hour Mon-Fri.

Another reason why we prefer a man who enjoys his job, is because if we end up in a serious, long-lasting, monogamous relationship, we don't want you quitting what you've put so much time and energy into. 401Ks and retirement funds are there for a reason-TWO actually!! You AND your spouse! Just because you go through a mid-life crisis doesn't mean you need to drop your responsible, yet boring desk job to become a marine biologist who travels to exotic places!

Finally, the part every guy needs to understand: why we are actually interested in what you make. It's quite simple! We want you to be fiscally sound! We want the alpha-male in our lives and for some of you, making a higher salary than your woman is going to make a difference. Truthfully, we really don't care if you make more or less than us, but we know how *you* feel about it; therefore, we'd prefer you make some dough.

Remember, when it comes to your job, we look at the big picture. If we ask the question, "Is that your wallet in your pocket or are you just happy to see us?" Don't answer by telling us how much you make. If you really want us to know you're loaded, be subtle. Try to master the art of being modest. It's a much more attractive quality. There are so many ways you can get our interest and give out clues to the amount of money you have. Need a one-liner? "My parents are republicans." Bam! You've made your point. But if your obnoxious attempt to impress us with your salary is evident, we will kick you to the curb. For all you know we make more than you. Who's your daddy *now*, Bitch?!?!?!

Bitch vs. Dick

What you shouldn't say:

"*Someone's* full of themselves!"

"I wish I had the courage you have."

What you should say:

"Is there anything you don't do?"

"You're hot stuff!"

A confident woman is a capable woman. These women come in rare form, and there are few and far between that are single. But if you happen to catch on and entice them to go out on a date with you, you'll know if you have one. A self-confident woman does not hide her qualifications. Instead, she flaunts them to let you know what you're up against. Then, the competition begins.

She may act like a bitch, but she's on top of her shit. She has a right to! And her ability to possess these bitchy qualities is what helped her get to where she is today. Now, if you're disgusted by her arrogance and not interested in seeing her again, then you're obviously not man enough for her. You see, a good match for this type of woman is someone who respects her confidence and has the same type of attitude. A match for this type of woman is someone who soaks up her egotism, chews it up and spits it right out at her. She's looking for her perfect match. Her perfect Richard. Pun intended.

Pompous asshole (PA)? It could work! It really depends on your charisma. If you're acting like one, just to show her up, she'll see right through it. She'll smell your weakness and choose the door's knob over yours. If you're a dick because you're bitter from being the short end of the stick your entire life, she'll also lose interest FAST! These types of guys disgust girls who have the ability to read people well. They instantly start wondering, what happened to this guy to turn him into such a little man? And now that we are mentioning "little men", yes Napoleon Complexes (NC) *do* exist. So if you are a man that suffers from this deficiency, please be aware women can detect this chink in your armor from a mile away. Whether it's the height or your cock that you are self-conscious about, or some other malfunction, your insecurity is discernable, so focus on getting over your anxiety. Cockiness is preferred. It's hot, it's challenging, and we know you've got some talents (hidden ones in your pants, preferably) if you're a true, cocky bastard. So, rock out with your cock in/out and bring 'em on!

If you are going to take the cocky route, be sure not to be a dick to *everyone*. People watching comments are fine. It's fun to make fun of people you don't know. However, insulting your server that has been working her ass off for the two of you, but lacks a brain or two is not the one that you should be commenting about. Be nice. She's working hard for the two of you. Know when to take pity. If a bum walks up to you and asks for money, pulling out a dollar bill, jiggling it over his head and demanding him to, "Dance, mother-fucker, dance!" *could* be funny, but your girl will probably get pissed at you because you're an asshole. Read your girl. Does she have a devilish side? If so, demand the damn dance! But nicely! If not, give him the plastic excuse and kindly keep walking.

Finally, the biggest reason why a confident woman will not follow through with a guy is if he's, once again, the nice guy. Guys who don't measure up to these types of women's potential are *extra* attracted to these Savvy Sallies. The attraction these men feel is so overpowering, they feel as though it's love at first sight. Unfortunately for them, it's not. It's more like infatuation at first sight, and it's one-sided. The reason why the personalities of powerful women are magnetic for weak men is because they absorb the positive energy coming from the women. They have such a good time with her on their date, they become addicted to their vigor and fall fast. You see, a confident, powerful woman may be considered a bitch, but that's not the only side of the icosahedron she reveals, especially on a first date! These types of women know how to have fun. If they're out with a Normal Norman (NN), they'll take charge of the date and make sure both he and she have a good fucking time! The weakling assumes her happiness is because she too, is having strong feelings towards him. He does not realize that she is just trying to make the best of a bad match. It is these ill-fated dates that make a man confused when he follows up with phone calls that go unanswered and then winds up complaining to his friends, "I don't get women."

The NN starts dreaming up reasons why his girl has stopped all communication. He becomes confused and drowns himself in assurances that she *will* get back in touch with him. *There's no way she's not interested! We had such a good time!* No, NN. Sorry to say, you're wrong. It was all an act. She didn't feel like dissing you to your face, but you weren't enough for her. Realize the rejection fast, and move on.

A woman who has this overwhelmingly positive power definitely wants the man to recognize it, but not necessarily acknowledge it. If she's being bitchy, she'll know how she's coming off. As a pompous asshole! Challenge it, but don't obey her for it. She does not want him to become dependent on her energy. CO-DOMINANCE! This is her goal. And yes, she wants a man to thrive off of her, but she has to be able to thrive off of him as well. If there's nothing for her to nosh off of, there will be no synergy. If that's the case, she's not going to stick around to judge the sexergy.

Meerkats

What you shouldn't say:

"I would never be able to spend a Christmas away from my family."

"My family gets together every Sunday."

What you should say:

"My family is drama free! I love it!"

"I'm really close with my family; although, we don't see each other very often."

Meerkats are sweet, innocent, little critters from the mongoose family. They live in groups with up to 50 family members. They create these maze-like burrows which they share with friends and family. And if you think living with fifty other relatives is intrusive enough, get this! Adult meerkats have actually been known to babysit others' young. FREE OF CHARGE! And what's even more amazing about these little mammals is their altruism trait. In order to keep an eye out for predators, meerkats take turns being the sentinel. What these means, is that one meerkat will go out and stand guard, putting themselves at risk, just to make sure the rest of the clan is safe. When they get tired, they tag the next victim, and that one takes its turn as bait. They are constantly risking their lives for their family. I know what you're thinking! Meerkats must be Italian! But no! They're actually African!

Is your family as close as a meerkat's? If so, hold back the information! Irish Catholics should pay extra close attention to this chapter. We know there are many of you, which means your family has drama and requires a lot of energy. Why can't they *just* use condoms!?!

Some things are thicker than blood. For instance...semen! Yes, your family might be the people you turn to if you need a donation of blood or a liver transplant, but hopefully you won't be exchanging your men at sea with them; and that's the bodily fluid your woman *wants* to deal with. So, make her number one-not your family.

Telling your woman that you get together every so often with your nuclear or extended family is great! A man who is close to his family members is a family man! And that is truly sweet. It automatically puts you in the long-term category, which in itself, is an excuse to sleep with you. If a woman's biological clock is ticking, or her eggs have already hatched, she's always on the lookout for a man who plays an active role in the family scene. Warning: involving yourself in family activities is one thing, but revolving your life around your family activities is another thing.

Let's discuss dysfunctional families. Isn't it funny how everyone claims they have one? There's always at least one black sheep to stir up some trouble. If you do, don't tell her. It's not the best way to market yourself. Just stay away from describing any negative family issues, unless it's something small, or something that you have nothing to do with that is taking place in another state that you rarely visit. A good adjective to use when describing your family is "low maintenance". If you choose to talk about the fam, tell her how happy they all are and about your lovely childhood growing up. Try not to start your conversation with, "Well, I'm from Missouri, and when I was five we moved to Virginia. At the age of eight, I walked home from school and found my mom dead on the couch, so my dad, little brother and I moved in with my grandparents in Florida. And I've been here ever since!" (True story. And guess if this guy got laid by the third date?)

The Checklist

What you shouldn't say:

"I usually only date blue eyed girls."

"I'm looking for a classy girl who is thin, and motivated to stay physically fit. Staying healthy is really important to me."

What you should say:

"I don't really have a "type" in the classical sense, but I'm looking for a woman that I can have an intellectual conversation with, who shares similar interests and is pretty much drama free."

"I want a girl who lives life to the fullest."

Everyone who has standards has a checklist. Does that mean that the one you're going to end up with, either in marriage or in bed tonight, is going to meet all of those criteria? Hell no! This checklist has been added to, flipped, switched around and altered throughout your entire life! It contains certain qualifications that you assume will generate your perfect mate. And you know what sucks? These checklists that we spend so much of our time mulling over are completely thrown out the window if you meet a person who lights the match for you. And yet, we continue to base so much of our dating lives on the attempt to fish for that perfect one who can mark all of the boxes. Are these lists realistic? Yes! But, are they required? Depending on how long or short your checklist is, maybe so... maybe not. One thing's for sure: there are certain things on your checklist that are more important than others. If the girl you are testing out over exceeds your exemplary expectations, but falls short of others, you still want her. For example, if your woman is super model-esque, intelligent and sweet, you might avoid the fact that she gets car sick and has to use other types of transportation to get from here to there. Before meeting her, someone may have asked you if you'd ever be able to date a woman who can't ride in cars, and your answer would have been, "Fuck no!" But after meeting your match, you begin to prioritize your prerequisites for your woman, and you think, "Eh, motion sickness might not be so bad!"

Women have checklists too! In fact, they are known to write these lists down and compare their pickiness. For some women, as they get older their checklists become more and more detailed, until they reach a point in their parabola where they begin to become so desperate that they actually start shortening the list by becoming less specific. Either way, they know how important the checklist is. And even though they too, have modified their list from time to time, they don't envision the list as an editable document. If a woman likes you, she *wants* to fulfill your needs and wants. She wants you check off every little detail of your list when you're with her and think in your head, "Jackpot".

Again, even though we all know it's not required to have every little thing checked off, you don't want to reveal to her that there is something that she is missing. She wants to be your type. So, don't start off with, "I usually date short girls," or "I've never dated an Asian before." If you do, she's going to think she's not your type and she'll start doubting the chemistry. Even if she feels it, she'll shy away from moving forward full speed, because you're dropping hints that she isn't what you're looking for. As a reaction, she'll automatically assume that you're not going to pursue her any further and her enthusiasm will die off quickly. So, if you get caught in a scenario, where your date asks what you're looking for in a girl, remain vague and don't mention qualities that you're normally attracted to if they don't pertain to her.

Whether your woman is or is not the type you normally go for, you don't have to point it out. Just remember to pick out her positive attributes and focus on them. Let her know you're impressed with what she has to offer and make her feel as though she's exactly what you're looking for. And when she mentions her odd ritual being able to whistle the national anthem without moving her mouth, you answer with a smile, "Wow! That sounds awesome!" Even though in your head you're thinking, "Oh my God, this girl's weird..." You externally reply, "Can you teach me how to do that?!?!?"

Wipe The Glass

What you shouldn't say:

"My last girlfriend dumped me....fucking bitch."

"I just moved into my new place three months ago. My ex and I didn't work out."

What you should say:

"One of my ex-girlfriends had this Golden Retriever, and I loved that dog. I'd like to get one of my own someday."

"My ex was a dentist."

This tricky topic can be ignored or discussed lightly. If an anecdote involving an ex-girlfriend can be integrated into conversation, general unbiased comments may be made. It won't threaten us to know that you have had an ex-girlfriend or two in the past. We hope you have! With this subject, you can't say too little, but you can *definitely* say too much.

There are many mistakes you can make when talking about exes. You can talk too much about one – this will make us think you are not over her. You can talk about too many – this will make us think that you have a horrible dating record. But the worst slip-up you could possibly make is letting us know you've had a recent break-up. None of us *want* to be the rebound. We've all done it. We've all been there! But unless you luck out and are dating a woman who is not looking for anything serious, you will not get laid once she realizes there is a chance you are not over your ex.

We don't even care if you were the one who caused the break-up! For all we know, she's still calling you every night, and that is one mess of which we don't want to be a part. If we detect an ex in the mix, it's over.

The truth is she will always be a threat. If you once found her attractive, you still do or at least remember the way she was, when you did. Those memories don't just fade away. If your ex-girlfriend was once hot enough for you to fuck, we fear that she might be as attractive, if not more, than we are and that causes us to instantly develop a complex. This is not good! If at this moment, you are imagining a cat fight between your ex-girlfriend and your new date, have fun with

29

that image, because that's all it's going to be. An early ex-girlfriend warning will make your new girl disappear quicker Osama Bin Laden.

Why mention my ex at all, you ask? We want you to have had a few serious girlfriends in the past. Otherwise, we automatically imagine you're bad in bed. The guys who have gotten to know our bodies the best and who made us open to trying new things are our ex-boyfriends. They *know* where the clitoris is! We want you to be able to push the right button, too. If you don't, we will not be too impressed. Our ex-boyfriends also know what positions work and which ones don't. The "Sarah Marshall Bridge" *is* physically possible, *if* you know what you're doing! Remember, we want a man in the bedroom who knows what he's doing, and a long-term relationship in your later past is excellent information to nonchalantly mention.

It's Not a Lie….If You Believe It

What you shouldn't say:

"Truth or dare."

"Do you want to play numbers?"

What you should say:

"That's a conversation for another day."

If you hear a hesitation-"You don't have to answer that."

Secrets. Everyone has them. Even the best, most functional couples keep secrets from each other. But here's something to keep in mind. Just because you don't tell something to the girl you just started dating, doesn't mean you're keeping secrets. Some conversations are just better left for a later date. For instance, try to imagine yourself as the girl in the following scenario:

A cute guy comes to pick you up at your front door. He's hot. You already want him and he hasn't even said anything yet. He opens your car door, and makes you laugh so hard during the drive over to the restaurant; you're concentrating on NOT peeing your pants. You're really enjoying dinner with him, and you notice how open the two of you are with each other. This makes you happy, because hey! The more you get to know, the more you like him! And that smile he flashes makes you want the clothes to melt off your body instantly.

After dinner, he suggests dancing. The two of you get carried away on the dance floor, and even though the music does not set the stage the penis polka, you can't stop thinking about how great he's going to be in bed. He grasps you and kisses you at the climax of a song, and just as the lights flicker to the beat, you find yourself lustfully falling.

(What you have here is an ideal situation where this girl is thinking this boy might be a potential suitor. She's turned on by him. She's attracted to his looks, likes his personality, and has a great time with him. Most importantly, she hasn't found anything that would make her think that he is a total disaster….**YET**.)

You begin walking home. He's holding your hand, and again, making you laugh at every corner.

"I really enjoyed tonight," he says. "How are you still single?"

(BIG MISTAKE! If you ever ask this question, it WILL be reciprocated. In this case, most people should lie and use the **only correct answer-**"I don't know. I guess I haven't found the right person yet." But in this case scenario, this guy has not learned how to keep his mouth shut. Let's see what happens...)

"I don't know... I guess I haven't found the right person yet," you reply. "How about you? Why are you still single?"

"Well, I haven't dated in a while." The man starts to dig his hole. Duhn duhn duhn.

"Why not?" You ask, as your steps begin to slow.

"Well, my last serious relationship ended pretty badly, and it has taken me a while to get back on my feet. She burned me pretty badly."

(Now, notice he didn't mention if it was a recent break-up, which you should have learned from a previous chapter is not something a girl wants to hear about. But he did leave the doors WIDE OPEN for her ask details. It's also obvious that this idiot is going to be truthful and answer her questions. As you read on, pay close attention to your thoughts as the girl-because remember, you're pretending to be her-and see how his chances of getting laid by you tonight dwindle....*FAST*.)

"What happened?" you ask.

"Well," he sighs. "I guess I can tell you, because I really feel as though we've made a connection tonight. I used to be married. And the bitch, Jen, cheated on me. And not just with one guy! With a few guys, I suppose. I don't even know. Anyway, it turns out she used my credit card for plane tickets to fly out and see them. There was one in California and one in Minnesota. There might have been one out in Florida too, but I think those were *actual* work trips. I'm sure she fucked the hotel's bellhop, if she could have actually have found one. So yeah, she left me in some debt, which I'm still trying to get out of. I actually had to declare bankruptcy but it's been a few years, so I'm finally getting on top of things."

DONE! I suppose I could tell you the ending in a nutshell. He walks her to the door, she does NOT invite him upstairs, and before he's off her doorstep she's already calling her BFF to tell her about this guy she just went out with and the brand of the suitcases he's carrying around.

Let's discuss his mistakes, shall we? When trying to get laid: A) Don't mention "our connection" with each other. If there is a connection, you'll both feel it. Don't get all sappy on her now. If you mention how close you feel to her on the first date, you're already letting on that you like her too much, way too soon. Leave some suspense! It'll keep her hanging around. B) You were married?!!?! Here are some possibilities that are going on through our head: You're online status didn't mention that! She doesn't want second dibs, especially since *she's* never been married. She doesn't even want to imagine what mom would say. Why the hell did they get divorced? *ARE THEY DIVORCED?* You basically just went from the sexy bachelor to damaged goods. Imagine how much you want a Kobe sirloin, cooked to perfection that has just been placed in front of you at a five-star steakhouse. Now, imagine what it looks like if it's never been cooked and has been sitting out in a dumpster for five days. Maggot infested? Yes. This is a great metaphor to use when describing how enticing a divorcé with a questionable separation is. C) If you've ever been cheated on-don't tell us right away. It means you weren't giving her what she wanted. Plain and simple. D) You declared bankruptcy? It doesn't matter if the girl's looking for a guy with money or not. Either way, your financial status is not acceptable.

I'm not saying LIE. I'm just making the suggestion to find ways to avoid mentioning your major downfalls. Use your brain, and stay away from topics of conversation that revolve around your past drama. If you have serious baggage from your past that you feel as though your significant other should know, tell her! WHEN YOU LABEL HER AS YOUR SIGNIFICANT OTHER! But, if you're just looking for a good lay, focus!!! Keep your suitcases closed. Simply put them in the overhead bin. If you think she might be relationship material for the future, wait until she falls in love with you. Give it three months. If things are good, she won't turn her back as quickly as she will from listening to an emotional guy unload his faggage on the first night.

FishingWithDynamite.com

What you shouldn't say:

"Online dating is for losers."

"Most of the women I've dated lately I've met online."

What you should say:

"I've never done it, but my friend seems to be pretty successful with it."

"At least it's an easy way to meet people."

Online dating. Everyone's doing it! These days, if someone is single they've at least searched one of those dating websites and checked out their options. Whether they've actually filled out a screen name and joined a site, is a different story. Either way, people are skeptical of the online dating services because there is still a stigma associated with it.

Throughout our generation, we've had negative connotations when it comes to personal ads in newspapers, 1-900 numbers that ended with SEXX, and even the scare of online sex offenders. Though the concept of online dating is more acceptable now, there are still men who whack off regularly while looking through girl's profile pictures. Even if we participate in online dating every once in a while, it's not something we're proud of. And if you've done it, it's not going to turn us on.

We probably won't admit to you that we have tried dating in Cyber Land if you ask, unless you are forthcoming with that information yourself. It's embarrassing! We don't want people to think we have to search through thousands of people online because we don't get out, or aren't social enough to meet someone in person. In our minds, online dating is a last resort, and it's not something that is easy for us to admit.

Not only do we not want you to know if we've tried online dating, we don't want you to be an online player either! It's a catch-22, we know! If you want to bring up the subject, it's your choice. But you better bet your sorry ass that she's tried it to, because if not, it might turn her off.

If you luck out and both of you have tried various sites, there might be a fun discussion ahead of you! Maybe she'll share the story of the guy with really small hands she went out with two weeks ago. You could enlighten her on the compulsive liar who kept changing her age that you dated last month! This experience may help the two of you bond together-but just remember one thing! The second you leave that date, go home and erase *any* online dating profiles of yours that she may have access to! If by any chance, she saw a side of you on your date that she was turned on to (i.e. sense of humor, charisma, or affableness), it may be expunged instantly when she see's your muscle picture taken by yourself through a mirror. Your personal information may make her lips curl in disgust. People convey information differently. What she may like in person, might not look so good in writing. And believe that if she really likes you, the first thing she'll do when she gets home is try to find a picture of you online to show her roommate. She'll by *Googling* the shit out of you.

If this *is* an online date, good for you! You are more than welcome to discuss the matter freely! Just don't make her think you are dating anyone other than her at the moment. She won't enjoy being "Wednesday" after you explain that you go out with an average of three girls a week. Also, don't get too heartfelt about what you're looking for in a woman. We do love a man who can communicate his feelings, but we're not looking for that on a first date. Remember, we are looking for a guy who can keep us on our toes and smiling at all times.

Looking for a good one-liner? Try this one. The line, "I'm just at that age where I don't want to meet a girl in a bar anymore," *does* intrigue us. Does that mean you are looking for something serious? Is this a witty remark men think we want to hear? Are you looking for a straight edged girl or someone who doesn't like to party? Does that mean you were once considered an alcoholic, but you are trying to cut back? But wait! We are in a bar at the moment-what does that *mean*?!?!?!

Joygasm

What you shouldn't say:

"Nice shoes. Wanna fuck?"

"Want to skip dinner and go back to my place?"

What you should say:

"You look fucking hot."

Nothing! Just do!

How many of you have ever had a catercousin? *"What the hell is that?"*-you may be thinking. Synonyms include: fuck buddy, friend with benefit, booty call, casual hook-up, one night stand-whatever! Well, if you're nodding your head right now, acting like an arrogant prick, guess what Jack Ass? Girls fuck for fun too!

We are *WELL* aware of the need for casual, hot sex. The reality is you'll never outdo our vibrators, but we get bored of the same position, image, music video, or porn scene that we replay in our heads when we get off. Like you, we appreciate variety when our will is to cum. Therefore, for many, the thrill and excitement of a good fuck is relevant to our existence.

IF (and yes, that is italicized and in bold) you are one of the lucky few that meets up with a girl that is just looking for a good fuck, you will have to learn how to make way for Pedro Paco, in order to put some sauce on her taco. In other words: don't **fuck** it up! Be sexy! Act cool! And make her want you in the bedroom. Otherwise? Adios mother fucker (ATM)!

Yes, this book is to get any woman in your dreams in your bed within three dates, but some of them are already reared up and ready to go! If you notice your date is rushing to get laid by stating she's really not hungry for dinner, and asking where you live, the pressure is on! Don't assume she wants to skip the date and fuck your brains out. Continue to escort her along your delightful evening, and don't fast forward, unless she bluntly says so. In the meantime, if you say or do something that's not attractive, or insinuate that you might be a disaster in the bedroom, she can simply turn her head at a 45 degree angle, zoom in on a new target, and be off! This can happen in a matter of seconds; perhaps, even before appetizers arrive! And here is something you should know. If you return from the bathroom and your date is quickly ending a conversation with another man, and gives you the excuse that he's an old friend-be leery. The two of them probably just exchanged phone numbers. If he was truly a friend, and she liked you, she'd make the introductions. She'd want to! On the other hand, it's not rare for a random admirer to waltz up to a woman when her date leaves the room to test the waters and see if she's still available. He'll know if she's interested fast, because her date's coming back! It could be ten seconds, or it could be three minutes-but he's wired to investigate the situation fast! If it does happen, it'll be a quick transaction, and if she actually does the number exchange with another man, you can pretty much kiss your chances good-bye! She has refocused her attention on someonenew, and if sex is what she is looking for, you're out of the running.

Sex is like pizza. Even if it's bad, you're still eating pizza! If your girl is in the mood for pizza, there's nothing stopping her. The question is: is she going to get the pizza from your pizzeria? It's your job to market the shit out of your pizza. And don't get too cocky too quickly. Know that until she pays for the pizza, she's not down to eat pizza (DTEP) just yet! Until you feel her grease on your sausage, keep marketing.

In summary, this chapter is ONLY for girls who are looking to get laid immediately. How do you know if you are lucky enough to have one on the line? Oh, you'll know... But don't let her know that you know. Wait until she demands it. Then, have a plan in the back of your head to whisk her away to a sexy enough setting to perform the sexual act. Chances are this girl isn't looking for anything serious. If that's the case, give her what she wants and voilà! You just got laid in less than three dates!!

Dutch People Are Ugly

What you shouldn't say:

"Are you treating?"

"Want to go Dutch?"

What you should say:

"Please..." (obnoxiously)

"What would you like to do next?"

The truth is Dutch people are not known to be ugly. In fact, they have a reputation of being beautiful **AND** amazing in bed! But if you think you're going to impress a girl by suggesting she chips in, you're sadly mistaken. Unless you don't give a shit about this girl, and **couldn't** care less about seeing her ever again, don't make a proposition that requires her wallet to make an appearance.

Just a side note, in case your date is not going well: if you or your date is not having a good time, you still need to shell out the money. There is no excuse in this matter. Things could always improve-you never know. But if you ask her to pay up early on, she'll know that you're not that interested and in that case lose interest in you. A girl who's bored on a date can't afford to pay attention-let alone pay for her half of the meal.

So now that we've determined you're paying, you still have to make sure you don't come off cheap. There are plenty of cheap dates that are acceptable first dates: a walk on the beach, a drink at a bar, coffee, etc. If you choose one of these as a first date, it is up to standard. But it must be followed up with a night on the town, planned and paid for by you. An independent woman might come off as if she likes making decisions, but the truth is she makes them all day long. She wants a man who can make some for her. Never ask a woman where she wants to go for dinner. You may ask what type of food she likes, but it's up to you to plan the evening. So, when she answers Thai, you can research the nearest Thai places near you and treat her to a posh place. Afterwards, you can ask her what she'd like to do next. The second activity of the night can be her choice. With the correct questions, you can make her feel as though she had a hand in planning the date, but you were really the one who molded the luxurious evening and made it happen! She'll secretly acknowledge that, and appreciate it as well.

What if your woman **has** money? There is a good chance your woman can pay her own way, or even treat for that matter! We don't care if it's obvious that she has more money than you. It still doesn't dispute the fact that you are the man and *you* are taking *her* out. Well, what if she asked *you* out? Doesn't matter. It *is* a double standard, and the whole "paying for dinner etiquette" is fucking with the evolution of women in this society! But it's just the way it is.

A powerful woman wants people to recognize her power. She will show off the money she makes, she will make her own decisions, and she will expect to be treated like a man. Since this is the case, you'd think that a woman wouldn't mind treating on a first date. And perhaps if you asked a few random women, some might lie and argue that they gladly would! But she'll instantly think you're not good enough for her, if you aren't the first one to whip the credit card out. The first three dates are an opportunity for you as the man, to show this woman that chivalry *does* still exist. It doesn't matter who has more money. She wants to be treated like a queen. It's not fair, we know. If a woman wants to live in a world where both men and women are treated equally, they should step up and act like a man! Ha, ha, ha. This is why they call "dating" a game! Women want their chocolate and eat it too! We know it's a contradiction, and we don't care. So pay up, bitch!

If your little lady offers to pay, deny her all the way. Whether she politely asks, or slowly starts to pull out her wallet when the bill comes, make her feel like she's an idiot for even thinking you'd allow her to pay a dime. A teasing look of disgust sweeping across your face will be enough, as you grab the check and slip your card into it. Also, make sure you place the bill on your side of the table, so she doesn't have a chance to slip hers in (in case she's persistently polite). If you need to verbalize something, simply say, "Please. Allow me!" It's genuine and to the point. She won't argue. You can also say, "my treat," but only if it's at the end of the date. If you mention it in the beginning while you're walking to your destination, she'll respond in her head, "Of course it's your treat! You're taking *me* out on this date!" You don't need to mention in the beginning that you're paying. Having our evening paid for is not an honor, it's an expectation. But again, if she's reaching for her purse, saying "my treat" while you pick up the check gives her only one way to respond. "Thank you," she'll say with a smile. Then, later she'll thank you in the bedroom.

And they say paying for a date *isn't* a form of prostitution. Psh!

The Robber or the Robbee

What you shouldn't say:

"Age means nothing."

"How old are you again?"

What you should say:

"They're the same age as us."

"The best musicians come from our generation! Don't deny it."

Sorry, boys. But age means *something*! Don't avoid the truth. But, if you think it's going to be an issue, then don't bring it up! Trying to negotiate why maturity doesn't matter is a waste of time. Don't try to deny that there is something improper with a couple dating who grew up in two different generations. The question is: will it work?

In America, it's natural for the female to be a few years younger than the male? Why? The answer is because we mature faster. We mature about three years faster, to be exact. So, that freshman girl who dated seniors in high school wasn't exactly a slut. She was just smart, and didn't like dealing with immature, adolescent fools. Don't hate.

The human brain stops maturing around the age of thirty. At this point, everyone begins to plateau, and what separates a mature person from another is their education and life experiences. Have you ever wondered why age difference doesn't matter so much to older people? It's because they are mature! Well, at least their brains are.

In your case, you're probably going out with a woman who is around the same age or a tad younger. If this is the case, excellent! Age should not be a problem for you. And if you're both close to the age of thirty, you're in the prime of your life and your brains are ripe! If this is your scenario, it's ok to mention age! Your age at this time in your life is important. Most people around the third or fourth decade of their life are getting ready for marriage and kids-two subjects of which your woman is bound to get you to talk about. I mean, come on! Once she reaches the age of 28, her egg stash drops down to less than 50%.

Quiet....

Do you hear it???

....

It's the ticking of the biological clock.... It DOES EXIST!

So do your best to tell a single woman in the prime of her life what she wants to hear. Find out if she's interested in marriage and kids. If not, have fun! But if she is, let her know there's a possibility the two of you could accomplish those dreams together. Ah... the happy ending she's been searching for.

If you're much older than the woman you are trying to lay, you have a choice. You can both flatter the hell out of her and pin her down faster than you could pin a tail on a donkey with both eyes wide open; or you can analyze and figure out why she's out on a date with you.

Daddy issues-It's probably what everyone is guessing. And when I say everyone, take a look around. Yes, all those people whispering about the hot girl and the older man named, Pedo? They're referring to you! You're a creepy old guy, and half the people are wondering if you're her dad or her date. Not only that, but you've just become a target for thieves. Because an older guy walking around with a younger woman *has* to be loaded, right? Just shower her with gifts, listen to her talk and don't mention *ANYTHING* that would remind her that you're the same age as your dad. Anything that would represent a large generational gap is a no-no. Subjects include music, presidents, past technology, movies, television shows, or any past year in particular. On a good note, you do have something that she's interested in, other than money (assuming you *have* money). Maturity. Dating an older man can be completely soothing for a woman. There's less drama, they make us feel safe, and they're experienced-in more ways than one! So, listen to her talk, give some advice and give her what she wants the most. Your attention.

If you are with a woman older than you are, she's a cougar...a fierce mountain lion, ranging from 75-225lbs, who hunts a variety of prey, including young men. She is either with you because her father fucked her up in the head, she has low self-esteem, or because she is simply bored with life. She likes you because you are hot and you're a youngin'. Your vibrancy makes her feel young at heart. So, be enthusiastic! Play the part! She's already made the decision she wants to sleep with you-not marry you. So, don't try and sit there and tell her how much you want to get married and have kids. She'll be thinking in the back of her

44

head, "Aw. You're so cute. And young! What the hell am I doing?" Just skip trying to impress her with a future, and instead, show her a good time! You don't have to work too hard to fuck the old bag. Just **don't** act too immature. That'll definitely make her rethink the whole robbing the cradle thing.

Game Off

What you shouldn't say:

"I'm so exhausted. I camped out for twenty-two hours this weekend, outside of *Best Buy*."

"Don't mind me. I have this blister on my thumb and it's just really annoying."

What you should say:

"I don't usually play video games unless my little brother comes over."

"The only hunting I've ever done is *Nintendo's Duck Hunt.*"

Whether it's *Sony Play Station 3, 2, or 1, Microsoft X Box 360, or Nintendo Game Cube*, don't try to boast about how quickly you've recently completed your campaign, or your online death to kill ratio. Your girl doesn't give a damn, and if she has had any experience with playing with video games recently, it's probably because she wasted her time playing them with the last dumbass, which she dumped once she realized he chose his *EA Madden* league over her.

Put your *Game Informer Magazine* away, Boys! If she asks you what your hobbies are, don't mention video games! And if you want to test her to see if she's totally against or ok with your video game madness, bring up the oldies, but goodies: the original *Nintendo, Sega Genesis*, and *Atari*. No girl has ever been able to resist a cuddly hedgehog or a two-tailed fox. She'll probably laugh it up, while reminiscing of sibling rivalry from years ago. P.S. If your girlfriend owned one of these consoles back in the day, it's a sweet gift to buy her for an anniversary/birthday/holiday. It's probably the easiest way for a man to be excused for bringing more videogames into the household.

As for the *Nintendo Wii*, there are three words that come to a woman's mind when they hear of a man who owns this gaming system. The first one is "pansy". It's not like videogames give men any masculinity points, but the *Wii* is definitely the most feminine of them all. Once again, *Zelda* was cool, back in the day, but you're older now, and most grown men have graduated to a larger battlefield. The second word is, "fatty". If you even mention that your exercising routine involves sporting it up on the *Wii*, you're going to look like a. . . (what's a better word than loser?) FUCKING LOSER. If your workout has been substituted for swinging your arms around while holding a five ounce controller, and you think that accounts for a sufficient enough workout, you're sorely mistaken. Go ride a bike, Lazy Ass. It exerts the same amount of low energy, but it will at least get you out of the house. This brings us to the final descriptive word: "pale". When picturing any guy who is obsessed with video games, a woman sees a pale skinned boy, sitting on the couch, in his pajamas, wrapped up in a fleece blanket with a mixing bowl filled with leftover cereal milk. Yum. That's what every woman wants. And if you didn't detect that sarcasm, you don't deserve to get laid. Hopefully, you own *Take 2 Grand Theft Auto*, because those prostitutes own the only ass you'll be getting anytime soon!

Fucking Like Rabbits

What you shouldn't say:

"So, when do I get to meet your kids?"

"What's their father like?"

What you should say:

"So, if I keep you out all night, will you be grounded?"

"Do you want to have (more) kids?"

When dating a woman with kids, you want her to know you're accepting of her kids and you have nothing against kids; but, not to the point that you're asking them to come along on the first date. She wants you to be into *her* first. Then, the kids will be invited into the picture. Otherwise, it's just creepy, and pedophilia-like (depending on what you say or ask). Wait until she brings them up, and then ask vague questions that aren't too personal. Asking about grades, sports, extra-curricular activities-fine. "Is their dad a big part of their lives?", "Do you get along with your ex?", "Did you go through natural childbirth?", "How's your teenager dealing with the whole puberty thing?"-not fine.

What if you're the one who has kids? If she doesn't have kids, don't talk about the kids! It's just not sexy to talk about kids throughout the whole date-make sure it's about you and her. If she wants to know more about your child(ren), she'll ask! Most importantly, don't bash their mother. It's a done deal. You're going to have to be attached to this woman for up to eighteen years. Everyone knows it! It's no secret! Just don't act like there's any unnecessary drama that will make your woman think twice about getting involved. At the same time, don't talk about the connection or unbreakable bond you'll always share with their mother because you parent the same child. Ew.

If both parties have been fucking like rabbits, you've both made your beds and now you must lie in them. Will your Brady Bunch fantasy come true? Maybe! But in the meantime, don't discuss a get-together. Awkwardness is bound to happen. You aren't getting married, so leave the kids out of it! Common ages, common activities, common personality traits may sooth the two of you into thinking there's a happy future. But avoid the day dreaming, and don't focus on the future. Focus on the present! Here you are...two adults, exhausted from working and raising your own families as single parents. You couldn't be in an easier position to get laid! Build a bond with your woman between the **two** of you! Let her think when she's with you, she's away from reality. The only issue you'll have is finding a location more romantic than the back seat of your cars.

Although it's best to not revolve your conversation around kids, if your woman wants to talk about them, listen. It can be a sensitive topic, especially if your woman hasn't dated much since she's entered the single parent world. No matter how much she wants to sleep around, there's more at stake and she'll be more reluctant. Showing an interest in her by listening to her stories and complimenting her amazing parenting skills, cushions the thought of having sex with someone new. Be that *Tempur-Pedic* pillow! Give her the support she needs, and help her sleep better...after you fuck her brains out!

One last, little piece of advice: No matter which one of you has kids, don't suggest any introductions within the first three dates.

Flooding the Basement

What you shouldn't say:

"I hate my life."

"My life is so overwhelming right now, let's just stick to yours…so what do you do?"

What you should say:

"I just stay out of it."

"I don't 'do' drama."

Drama is annoying and undesirable. As people age, it becomes even more annoying and undesirable. A woman is not going to be attracted to you if you have a lot of overwhelming commotion going on in your life. She has her own crap that she needs to deal with, and she's in search of a man who can lend a shoulder and a cock; a shoulder for support when things get rough and a cock for pleasure, so she can get her mind off unnecessary woes. If a guy has his own shit that he's constantly tied down with, she's not going to want to get involved with him and his luggage. And if this is the case, there is absolutely no way he's going to come off as a secure man who will make his lady feel safe by being her rock through hard times.

With this in mind, if you have drama in your life, try not to talk about it on the first date. Depending on how serious it is, it is very possible that she will think you don't have your life together; therefore, won't foresee a secure future with you. It doesn't matter if your basement flooded from the storm the night before and insurance is claiming they aren't responsible. Those details might be flooding your head, but don't let them flow over to hers. Telling someone about the negatives in your life does not help build a good first impression. You don't want her going home to make the inevitable phone call to her best friend and say, "He was great, *but* he's having issues with his job-and it sounds like he's not going to be there much longer." The best friend will tell us how much of a soon-to-be unemployed loser he is and urge us to move on. And best friend advice regarding men is usually taken when the relationship is in the beginning stage. It's not until the girl has fallen for the guy that she tells her BFF to fuck off.

If it's little drama, such as your friend is sleeping on your couch, or your little sister, once again, is asking you for money, it might stir up some interesting conversation. Venting is healthy, and it can sure as hell be fun for the two of you. Venting about little shit won't make a vein pop out of your head, or cause your palms to sweat. It could possibly provide excellent conversation and help the two of you get to know each other better. Just make sure your drama makes you look like your stable and have control over the situation.

If she has drama, remember you're here to get laid. It doesn't matter if you don't give a shit about whether or not her cat is getting a full night's sleep. Listen and be supportive. A woman not only wants a good listener, but a friend who will empathize with her issues. One of the number one misconceptions men have of successful women is we want a problem solver. We want to solve our *own* problems. We just want someone to listen to us vent and bounce ideas off of. When you're with a woman who is venting, provide options. She'll appreciate the attempt; but, she has already considered them. Don't pity her or try to act like it's going to be a tough situation. She's a grown woman, and she'll figure it out. Lastly, be positive. Someone who helps a woman look on the bright side makes her smile. Positivity makes people want to be around you, and if you're making a woman feel good about herself, and helping her build confidence to attack the issue at hand, she'll be more likely to want to talk more about it with you in the future.

Stay focused and be her rock, or shall we say stone? In return, she'll give you a place to put your sword. You want her to think that when she's with you, she won't have to worry about drama-*your* drama, to be exact. A woman will not attach herself to a man who can't get his life together after the age of 25. She wants her partner to make her feel safe, secure and stand behind her even when she's wrong. Haven't you heard the lyrics to that *Train* song? Remember, in the beginning of a relationship, a woman will not want to continue seeing a guy who has problems. No matter how hot you are…(scratch that). *Most* of you are **not** hot enough to be worth the energy a woman would need to exert on your disorganized life. **No** girl wants to date a mess. So shave your face, shave your balls, clean your house and clean your thoughts.

Netjobbing

What you shouldn't say:

"I'm an entrepreneur."

"I have an internet business."

What you should say:

"I work in marketing."

"I own a business. We deal with ..."

"Make up to $100,000 per year from your home!" We've all seen these advertisements before that only an unemployed loser would ever investigate any further.

In a woman's mind, the word "entrepreneur" means unemployed. Yes, you may have plenty of drive, but exactly *how many* businesses have you ever tried to conquer, but have been unsuccessful with? "Well, the economy was bad, I couldn't get any investors, it just wasn't the right time for the product...."

Yeah...

Tell us more about your life's failures.

We agree, we are in the age of the internet. Without it, one cannot be successful. But think of how many starving artists scrounging around on the streets in NYC, and how many amateurish actors/actresses are giving blow jobs in L.A., in hopes of a part as an extra. These numbers are *NOTHING* compared to the amount of computer geeks with a degree in programming, trying to start their own online business. Unless you have an innovative, new idea, implement it at precisely the perfect time, and Gate's connections, you're probably not going to be a triumphant capitalist. So stop pretending your garage band's going to make it and come to terms with reality, Bud. You have a bachelors degree, have a hard time working for other people because you think you're better than the entry level position they hired you for, and you're eager to make money fast. Being the impulsive, wishful thinker you are, here's one thing you're not-rational.

But we think it's cute that you give such rational thought to such an irrational idea, Mr. Entrepreneur.

Retiring by the age of forty is a nice dream, that your woman will enjoy sharing with you. But if you're one of the men that *actually* think it's going to happen, she'll doubt you and feel horrible about it. Remember, we want a man who has a stable career. We don't care if you become a multi-millionaire just in time to spend all of your money during your mid-life crisis. Remember, the amount of money is not what we're most interested in. We're more concerned with stability and contentment. So, if you're in a period of your life where you're trying the internet avenue, remain realistic, and most importantly: don't make her think you're struggling financially. Talk about a future vacation you and your boys are taking. Perhaps mention that you're car hunting. Don't bother telling her what *type* of car you're looking for. Just the fact that you're in the market for a large product will ensure her that you have money coming in.

In conclusion, if you're one of those guys that are proud of their technologically advanced occupation, be sure that your date will not be as impressed as you think she'll be. When she asks you what you do, don't answer with your full job title. "I'm a multi-level marketing agent for a mobile company," will make her think that even *you* don't know what you do. Generalize, Men. "I work in marketing," will do. Or "I have my own business." If you don't have insurance, a set salary, or a stable enough job that you know will still exist in five years, avoid detailed conversation. Just tell her how much you love your job, and act like you live comfortably. And please…stop pretending. If your business meetings take place in a coffee shop instead of a corporate board room, it's not a business that will impress your woman.

You, Yourself & Yours

What you shouldn't say:

"I don't think you understand! Let me explain further!"

"I know this story seems drawn out, but you need to hear all of the details in order to *get* the punch line!"

What you should say:

"That's awesome! So, (reiterate what she just told you in your own words). Right?"

"No! Keep going! This is quite entertaining!"

When it comes to taking turns in conversation, don't come off as if you're a seagull. You don't need to be the bully of conversation. Just because a female is attracted to a dominant male, doesn't mean you have to dominate the conversation. So, take it back a notch if you've been known to be a little chitty chatty.

If your girl is a better listener than talker, it's because she's already made the decision that you're never going to see her again and doesn't want to put forth the effort in discussion, or maybe she's sweet and purely interested in what you have to say. In either case, she really doesn't need to hear the nitty-gritty details of your job. If the girl shuts you up and straightforwardly asks, "Do you work with *words* or *numbers*?" Simply give her a one word answer, shut up and move onto the next subject. That's her nicely, put way of saying-*hey. I really don't give a shit. Just sum it up for me, please.*

Dating is like interviewing. Your potential future boss is not going to ask you for details of something he/she doesn't care about. They have a busy day and they know within the first five minutes if you're in the running to get hired anyway. The same goes for dating. She wants to hear the highlights. Then, when you hit a bullet point she's interested in hearing more about, she'll specifically ask you for the details.

Problems with silence? This is an interesting, and delicate situation. Long bouts of silence usually bring awkwardness to at least one party involved. But if you're quick to fill in the silent gaps with clumsy nonsense, she'll notice you have an issue with silence and sense your nervousness. Remember to remain calm, and transition smoothly. If there's a seemingly long break of conversation, don't ask a silly question to replace the stillness. Blurting out, "So! Do you have any siblings?" is going to come across as if you're running out of topics to discuss and you're trying hard to fill in the pauses. You don't want her to think you're putting too much effort to keep the conversation going. One of the recipes for first date butterflies is to have conversation flow effortlessly. So if the silence occurs, look around your physical setting and make a comment. Bring her attention to a physical object to refocus her. Don't search the blank slate in your head for a comment. Take her mind off of the silent state and put it on something else. Giving her a visual will readjust her thoughts.

Here's the easy part. Remember to ask about *her*. Women are known to talk **a lot**. Remember how chit-chatty your mom was on the kitchen phone when you were younger? Women are good at communicating and love to do it! So, let her! If an hour's gone by and the only thing you've determined about her is that she's from Missouri and her parents just retired recently, you're babbling too much. Be aware of it! Talking too much is a dating defense mechanism. If you notice the wpm ratio is 10,000:200, ask more questions. Let her take the floor.

Your New Haircut

What you shouldn't say:

"My last girlfriend was a fucking skank."

"I'm of Italian descent."

What you should say:

"I'm not a big fan of techno."

"I hate putting shit in my hair."

Even though this book is distributed outside of the Tri-State area, this chapter is dedicated to pathetic Italian, or Italian-wannabe, guidos. The rest of the world has a right to know. Unlike lucky leprechauns, they DO exist! They can generally be found in New Jersey, Brooklyn, Long Island and Staten Island areas. In daylight, they venture out to areas such as construction sites, Italian restaurants and other small, family-owned businesses. During the evening, you can find them swarming gyms and grunting like an old man during a prostate exam. And at night time, you can always spot hundreds of them fist pumping at the Jersey shore. They're the ones dancing off beat with the greased back hair and tight-ass shirts. Maybe if you're lucky enough, you'll spot *MTV True Life*'s Tommy searching for his cheesebawlls.

It's hypothesized that guidos think so highly of themselves because of one well-known and much loved guido. This man is of course, Rocky Balboa. It is true that Rocky has stolen the hearts of many women, but come on! He's Rocky! Can *you* beat the Russian? Doubtful. So stop acting like you can outrun Apollo Creed on the beach, run up a snow covered mountain, or eat lightning and crap thunder.

The funny thing about guidos is they think they are every woman's dream! Maybe when we were younger we desired the dark hair, dark skinned man, but then we became experienced and found that the more Italian the man, the smaller the dick. Men, no matter how many buttons you undo, or how white your wife beater is, you need to stop strutting around as if you're hot shit. Women LOVE confidence. But we also know an asshole when we see one. If you spend the whole date insulting everyone you come into contact with, your girl will not be impressed. Even if you treat everyone like shit, but put her on a pedestal, she will spend most of the evening feeling sorry for everyone you've spoken to/about. Remember, women have a nurturing side, and no matter how much you treat us like a queen, we don't want to be with a man who doesn't respect others.

Keep in mind, discussing how much money you have compared to everyone else in the world *is* disrespectful. It's nice when a guy's rich, but we don't want him to flaunt it. The worst is when an Italian *doesn't* have a lot of money, but they act like they do. They like to brag about how much their *Lexani* rims cost on their old, used-but, supped up car. It's similar to how they like to brag about their "beach house", when in fact, they're chipping in over a thousand dollars to own a corner of a crappy shore house because the rooms packed with two bunk beds and a cot are already called for. All this time, they fail to mention the fact that they still live at home with Ma.

Ok, let's say you're Italian but don't consider yourself a guido. "This chapter is so true," you're saying to yourself right now. "If anyone hates guidos, it's me! They're a disgrace to our relatives." See, right there is a turn off. Just how women don't get turned on by Jewish men who want Jewish women, we don't get turned on by a man who acts like Italians are the elite. You are not a part of the mafia. And just because your friend's cousin married into a family of a guy who knows someone who met Frank Costello, doesn't mean you are important. Just because some Italians were smart enough to get involved with some garbage, doesn't mean they *aren't* garbage.

If you're still confused, consider this. Do we introduce ourselves and state our heritage? No. Who gives a damn which country our great-great grandparents came from? The only time it will ever be brought up is when our kids are doing their third-grade family tree project. It's just not important!

If you are a guido and this is your first encounter with the true disgust women have for your kind, don't fret. Just remember what annoys us and try to avoid talking about your Italianesque. Yous guys have to stop seeing it as a point for you and notice it as a point against you. So whether you're Snookin' For Love or you're best friends with The Situation-get it straight, guys! WE DON'T GIVE A FUCK if you are Italian!!! What we really need to focus on are some new slogans. We need to create some new t-shirts. How's this idea? "Italians *ain't* stallions!" And then in really tiny print underneath add, "Jagerbombs..."

Fine Wine

What you shouldn't say:

"I was that kid with the light sticks at every dance (followed by an arm shuffle)."

"I remember getting a wedgie my freshman year of high school. It sucked."

What you should say:

"What were you like back in high school?"

"College was the best time of my life!"

When it comes to the fascinating alchemy of aging wine, it is known that wine improves with age. In order to enjoy a savory glass of wine, one must let it age. The longer you wait for it, the better it tastes. Like a bottle of wine, we care about your present stage, not your past. At this point in time, we are trying to learn about the man you are today; we don't need to hear all about the gawky stops along the way.

High school and college are critical time periods when people discover their personal identity. Although you are a completely different person now than you were back then, stories from these past times may be detrimental to our vision of you. You have to be careful when describing yourself in the past, because you don't know how she will perceive your simple narratives.

Swirlies, body odor, lice, wedgies, one hitter quitter, trailer park trash, emo, MJ's one white glove, break dancing, *McDonald's* cashier-these terms will probably not make her jump for joy. The words, "Aw! That's cute," followed by a diffident giggle is not good. It is her being kind. At that moment, she is picturing you at a young age, as an awkward pubescent and is pitying you. Do you think girls want to sleep with men they pity? **No.**

Although the chess or golf team may be acceptable, it's best not to focus on those as your best attributes. There is a chance that she may picture you with the pepperoni-pizza faced academic club. Think of the guys who got the girls back then. They were the ones that gave us wet dreams (and they still do)! Even ten or twenty years later, *they still are!* Don't tell her you used to look like Billy Bob from *Varsity Blues!* We don't want Billy Bob! We want Lance!

We don't want to know about that one time, when you were the band geek. Don't tell us your friends call you the "Triple Crown" because you used to have a problem with 1) impotence, 2) lasting more than three pumps, and 3) being too small. Later-*MUCH LATER*-If we ever meet them; you can explain the legend behind the grand epithet, although some things are better off left unsaid.

Have you heard the story of the three-finger boy? When the girl went to jerk him off, his dick was smaller than her hand. In order for her to have room to perform the sliding motion, she could only use three fingers. It's called juvenile penis, Boys. If this is you-keep it to yourself! When we're in bed with you, we won't be walking out because of the size of your penis, although if we find this information out ahead of time, you won't be escorting us anywhere!

These things are cute after we fall for you. We want a guy who can look back and laugh at himself. But women are quick to judge a book by its cover. If at any time during your introduction, we relate the thought of you to a bad memory it may create a stigma. Help us focus on you now, and not back then!

Condom Sense

What you shouldn't say:

"Pretty much everyone I know has an STI. It's really no big deal."

"Yeah, well if you have herpes, you only have to take medicine when it flares up. It's really not that bad."

What you should say:

"My friend's girlfriend *somehow* caught herpes after dating him exclusively for two years. It sucks to be him."

"Yeah, I stay away from STIs."

Condoms suck! We know! Women actually feel less too, and those *Ribbed for Women Trojans* suck ass. Don't think we enjoy them any more than you do. What we do enjoy is a clean dick, and keeping our snatches clean as well. If you slip it between her thighs, condomize!

What guys need to realize is that women are horny! But smart women make smart decisions. Because we do not want to be labeled as a slut; the chances that we *just* sleep with you are slim. We need to validate our choices with justifications that we actually believe and consider reasonable. If we choose to have sex with you it has to be on *our* terms and comforting to *our* feelings. We need to make sure that you aren't using us for a night and in case you are, you don't have any diseases you're going to pass on. So for our sake and yours- cover your stump, before you hump!

A girl might throw out the idea of STIs just to see your reaction. (STI is the new STD. Nowadays, it's politically correct calling it infection, rather than disease.) For your sake, this could be one of two reasons: 1) She wants to try to figure out if you have one from your reaction, or 2) She *has one* and she wants to see how disgusted you look when the thought pops into your head- so beware! Don't go crazy if she does bring up the subject. If she works in the medical field or as a social worker, it's probably going to come up in conversation only because it's one of the most interesting topics she can bring to the table. Just roll with it and don't give her any reason to think that your crotch is covered in cauliflower-like warts. Wrap that dick in foil, before you check her oil!

If she brings up a story of a fellow friend with an STI, silence or an uncomfortable vibe from you will make her question your health. If you present a story of "your friend" with pity and a little humor, she should believe that you're really talking about a friend and not you. Be sure not to move onto another topic until her facial expression reads that she is relieved. STIs are no joke, so be sure to wrap before you poke!

Pregnancy is another reason why you need to use a condom. Unless you are on a date with some crazy psycho, she is not going to want to get pregnant within the first three dates. Keep in mind, the average sperm count per load is a few hundred million! It only takes one of those suckers to make its way up her tube. Don't take any chances! For all you idiots out there, if you accidently put a condom on your dick the wrong way, don't just flip it and put it back on. GET A NEW ONE! Also, make sure to remove the air and leave room at the reservoir tip-if not, it can pop! Then, she'll be popping out your baby in 9 months! Finally, for those of you who think its ok to have a couple of unprotected pumps, it's not. I don't care if you think you have ESP, YOU CAN'T FEEL PRECUM ALL OF THE TIME! I apologize for the lesson on applying condoms, but these are the reasons that condoms aren't 100% effective all of the time. It's not necessarily the condom's rate of failure, but the idiots who wear them! Don't be silly. Protect your Willie!

Abortion? Don't even bring it up! It's ok to have a conversation about having kids one day. But if you're curious what her thoughts on abortion are keep it to yourself. This is not a conversation we want to have when we're debating on sleeping with you or not. It's too easy for you to say something that will upset her. Just USE A CONDOM! Don't be a loner and cover that boner!

The Other Woman

What you shouldn't say:

"I'm high right now."

"I have to make a quick stop after dinner to do some business."

What you should say:

"In college, I got by living off of beer, pot and *Ramen Noodles*."

"Have you ever gotten high and listened to Pink Floyd's 'Dark Side of the Moon' during the *Wizard of Oz*? You've got to match it up!!!"

Her name is Mary Jane. You think about her 24/7. She makes you horny. You don't mind sharing her, because...well? When you're around her, you're just not the jealous type. She has a way of comforting you. You're willing to spend money on her. She entices you with her smell. You like it when she sparkles. She doesn't bitch, complain or stress you out in any way. You love her. She's your girl.

Brownies, anyone? This may be a lovely dessert you'd like to share with your new girl, but this is not something we want to know about straight off the bat. Will we judge you if we find out you are a fan of pot? Not necessarily... Hey! Maybe we're interested in having a heated discussion on whether or not it should be legal. It's a good topic to converse about. It brings up good stories as well.

How can you use this topic as an advantage? Please read the following:

My cousin was high off his ass one time. He and his friend went to Red Lobster for the all you can eat Lobsterfest. My cousin asked the server, "What's the record?"

She's like, "What?"

"What's the largest amount of lobster one person has ordered?" he asked again.

"I don't know," she answered. He asked to speak with the manager, who also did not know the answer. Finally, my cousin demanded to speak to the head chef.

"21 lobsters," the chef answered.

"Then let's begin the process!" yelled my cousin. "I'll take 22!" So his friend sat there for over 5 hours until my cousin finished his dinner. I'm sure he didn't shit right for a week.

Tah-dah! With a humorous story, you have just created a good laugh and an opening for her to try to outdo your story. Notice the disgusting stoner story does *not* involve you! It involves someone else, so if she is judgmental of the herb, you'll be able to catch her reaction early on.

You see, back in college marijuana was a part of everyone's lifestyle. If we weren't labeled chronic potheads back then, we at least tried it once or twice. Our main concern, and Boys-please pay close attention to this: the truth is we don't want you smoking it anymore.

Here's the deal though. As long as you're not dependent on it, we won't complain. If you're thinking you've had girlfriends in the past who have completely accepted your love of weed, think again and answer this next question. Why did you break up with her? Was she interested in taking your relationship to the next level? Did she want to get more serious? A three-foot bong is not an attractive display on your coffee table. Were you not putting enough energy in the relationship?

Plain and simple: when a woman first realizes that a man's favorite holiday is April 20th, she becomes concerned. She automatically feels that the chances are high (pun intended) that you suffer from depression or laziness, and have absolutely no goals in life. What about marriage and kids? If that's what is on your woman's mind, she plans on moving forward, and at a faster speed than your sorry, high ass.

Aspiration? More like Masturbation!

What you shouldn't say:

"I'm an aspiring actor."

"I'm writing a book."

What you should say:

"I'm a freelancer."

"Hi, I'm Johnny Depp." (But this supposedly only works *if you are* Johnny Depp.)

For most employed people today, their aspirations are more like dreams, rather than short-term goals. "One day..." What really ends up happening is they spend their free time finding ways to relax, or get off. Very few people stay true to their hopes and dreams, and if they do, it's because they have found a way to turn their aspirations into their hobby, and over time have attempted to accomplish their goals. Think of it this way: how many people in this world aspire to do something better and more exciting with their lives? How many of those people actually accomplish those goals in their lifetime? Now think: how many times a day do those people masturbate?

(If only they could take the amount of time they spent jacking off and put it towards something useful!)

Notice, how calling yourself a "freelancer" (another word for unemployed), is preferred over telling your woman you're "an aspiring actor". That's right, Boys. Your woman would rather hear you're unemployed than hear about your dramatic talent. What do you think your woman would rather tell her friends? She's dating someone in between jobs, or an actor? The first thing they'll ask is, "Oh! What has he been in?" It'll be followed by an awkward silence. *That's* how bad it is to tell your woman you're an actor. We don't care if you have an agent or a publicist. You're *much* more inclined to landing a REAL job, than a commercial anytime soon.

It's just like when you were little, and you aspired to be a marine biologist. Did you make that dream happen? No. You took another route. Unless you take the time, energy and are committed, aspirations are nothing more than small talk that could eventually make you go awol during your mid-life crisis.

The sad part about aspirations and goals is that the harder they are, the less support you get from your friends, family and women. No one wants to support your dream of becoming the next contestant on *Hell's Kitchen*, when you're an accountant at a big-time law firm, making bank. What, do you think your boss is going to 'ok' your time off? As if you didn't think he could be worse than Chef Gordon Ramsay....why don't you go ask him and see how he reacts? The truth of the matter is no one wants to be supportive until you've made it big! Once you've shown some success, then you can start claiming your fame, and telling people you're trying to be an actor, artist, singer, songwriter or whatever.

Seriously, don't even bring it up. The first thing she'll ask is for proof so she can *Google* That Shit (GTS) when she gets home. And if you have nothing to show her, you'll look like a tool. You might as well be unemployed and have your credit card max out at the dinner table. This book will be of no use to you. It's *just NOT* going to happen.

Do you know how many aspiring actors are roaming the streets of LA and NYC right now? We sure as hell don't. But, you can bet your ass that there are tens of thousands. And if you're confident, and think that you are one of the most talented of those tens of thousands of people, good for you! But you do realize that doesn't even matter...what matters is who you know, and being at the right place, at the right time. And with that in mind, it makes your chances slim, Jim. On the bright side, if you are aspiring to act, you probably have a pretty face. So use that to your advantage and maybe you'll get a good luck fuck.

Junk in **Your** Trunk

What you shouldn't say:

"What, these marks on my arm? Aww.... They're nothing."

"I try everything at least once."

What you should say:

"I've never done any serious drugs."

"I don't do drugs."

Drugs are bad. But it's true that everyone has their own "drug" that helps them get through the day. Whether it's coffee, candy, TV, alcohol or cocaine, you should really try to wean yourself off of it. But if your drug of choice is something you can't buy in a store, you have issues. So, don't let her know of it.

Even if your experimenting days are over, there's no need to bring up the past. Any NA, AA or past rehab experiences you *or* a family member has "overcome" should not be brought up. Your drug snorting history is not something that's attractive and if you mention to your date that you did a little blow, it will blow your chances of getting a blow job. You're not Johnny Depp and instead of brushing it off and focusing on your positive attributes, she'll be trying to get a peek up your nose every chance she gets, to see if you still have a septum.

So, if you're Mr. Try-it-all, don't let her know you're open to new things. New things in the bedroom? Perhaps. But trying a drug once doesn't usually work, considering you can get hooked on the first crack. Yes, it is quite the contradiction that pot and alcohol aren't included in this chapter, but for some reason they are socially acceptable. The odd thing is, a woman wants a man that is familiar or has tried pot and alcohol, but who has never tried any other sort of drug. Considering college life is a whirlwind of sexual and drug-related experiences, you'd think that a woman who wants an educated man would be accepting of his druggie past. But, no. She does not want to hear about your walk down Shakedown Street. She does not want to know stories about how your Uncle Sid used to tell you scary stories about the shadows in the night. And finally, she does not want to hear about your old best friend. It doesn't matter how much of a fun guy he was, if you swarm her with these bygone tales, she'll wonder if you're ever going to do them again, and if so, how often?

If you really must let her in on your little drug habit, mention your bands of choice. A man who talks about his love of Bob Marley obviously smokes pot every once in a while, but hopefully not every six hours. A hippie-loving, concert-goer that makes every effort to see a Grateful Dead or PHISH cover band is sure to have done some crazy shit in order to experience the "ultimate high". Beyond your list of live, psychedelic concerts that you've hit up in the past, do not go into further detail down memory lane of your trips. Unless these "trips" consist of palm trees and margaritas, your woman is not going to be turned on by hearing you express all of the times you almost overdosed on some exotic bleach ingredients.

As for prescription drugs? Not much better, Pill Popper! It's no excuse that our country makes up almost half of the pill popping population of the world. Thanks to Reagan's policy which gave permission to pharmaceutical companies to advertise, everyone in this country, whether healthy or not, thinks there's a pill to solve their problems. If you're wacked out on prescription drugs, we want no part of it. It doesn't matter if you tore your ACL in a masculine, football tackle. If you're still mouthing oxycodon, you're a basehead. Face it, you're a junkie. Perhaps a more rich and educated one than the average meth head, but you're still a junkie. This book's goal is not to help people get off drugs, but that's ok! We can kill two birds with one stone! Let this be your wakeup call and get help! And remember…keep your little drug habit your little secret. I'm not saying wear your *D.A.R.E.* t-shirt. It would probably be a little too tight; taking into account you haven't worn it since eighth grade, but make it aware that you stay away from that shit!

Gasparilla

What you shouldn't say:

"I'm kind of claustrophobic. I really don't do well when there are a lot of people surrounding me."

"I wouldn't say I'm a couch potato, but I'm definitely a homebody."

What you should say:

"Have you ever been to Gasparilla! My college buddies and I go every year. We just throw one huge party! It's crazy-fun!"

"You've never been to Fantasy Fest? What, you don't believe in public nudity?"

Perhaps the good men from the *Little Peckers* could clue you in on how to lay a woman at Gasparilla, but this isn't very hard considering everyone is sloppy drunk; therefore, everyone is smushable. Gasparilla is a Tampa Bay event that includes a parade, boats, nakedness, drunkenness and pirates. It is the Mardi Gras of the western coast of Florida and is filled with people fucking, doing keg stands and puking on neighbors' front lawns. And don't forget the pissing. Yes, there's *a lot* of pissing on those front lawns.

If the most exciting annual event that you attend is your high school/college reunion every few years, you better find some new action. Small town, communal events do not count either. As for annual drunk fests? As long as they're not local, they count as a vacation! Anything that includes a road trip ensures out of control fun. The summer carnival does not equal vacation status. But, driving a few hours to HalloWeekend, is an escape from reality. And those crazy-expensive evenings/weekends you plan on attending, will make you more attractive.

A woman who works hard knows how to party hard. Going to a high end club every couple of weeks will not satisfy her thirst to party. She wants to look forward to things. The chances that you have enough money to fly her to Tahiti once a month are slim, so use these crazy-fun events to your advantage. You want your woman to think you have one vacation-like experience *at least* once every three months. It will make her think you're FUN, FUN, FUN! It will also make her think that you are well-liked by others. People who have a lot of friends, have a lot of party rituals. This is extremely attractive.

Are these exciting events going to make your woman think you have a drinking problem? Hell no! Instead, she's going to think you're a fun guy and know how to maintain a steady party life in your older age. A woman loves to see her man have fun! A man who gets all riled up about these events is going to show her a fucking good time. But just because you attend these events with your friends doesn't mean you're the life of the party. (And keep in mind everyone wants to date the life of the party. **They want to sleep with them too.**) She doesn't want a man who shows up, but mopes around waiting for it to be over. If you take pride in these fun festivals, let her know! If you dress up like a ratty ol' pirate-tell her! Yes, she'll think you're a fucking idiot, but she'll laugh and find your confidence and enthusiasm extremely sexy.

100-300 Yards

What you shouldn't say:

"Have you ever dealt with a restraining order?"

"I think cops have the right to kick the shit out of criminals."

What you should say:

"I don't remember the last time I got really worked up."

"Wrestling is gay."

Scars can be hot. They're somewhat like tattoos, because they're permanent and have a story to go with them. On a side note, if you have a tattoo of a cartoon character, or some lame tribal sign that you got on some random, drunken night, hide it. A cartoon character tattoo is not only a turn-off, but you'll take the place as the number one loser to talk about during your date's 'girl's night out'.

But let's try not to digress here. If you have a scar, and it piques your date's interest, tell her the story of how you got it. Fib, if you want. She'll know it, and think it's cute. If you want to claim you were shot, gnawed on by a shark, or got into a fight, go for it! Obviously, your next line would be, "But you should see the other guy/shark..." This line is cute, but if she asks for details about the so-called fight that you were visibly losing at one point during the brawl, **don't** lead her to believe this fight happened in your adult years, or much worse, recently. A guy who used his fist to think with was hot in high school, but after you turned 18 and became legal, battery is a completely different thing. Guys go to jail. Women go to psychologists. We don't want a man who can't deal with his problems in a nonviolent way. So when you pull up to Taco Hell and they get your order wrong, don't mention that you'd like to rub the cashier's face up against the cheese grater.

A woman who has her head on straight stays clear of psychotic behavior. They know of *Jerry Springer* because they watched it for comedy, not to relate, or to improve their self-esteem. A woman who stays in an abusive relationship is not weak. A woman who *enters* an abusive relationship, is weak. Signs of

71

unhealthy/abusive relationships pop up early. This is when a smart woman will instantly choose to diverge onto another pathway (or shall we say into another man's bed).

In order to assure your woman that you do not have a violent streak, avoid the following issues: restraining orders, knowledge of dog fighting, wrestling, martial arts, fighting experience, or bitch slapping of any kind. If you are surprised and take pleasure in one of the above subjects listed, *what the fuck is wrong with you!??!?!* (P.S. Wrestlers who simply wrestle or kick box because they are passionate about the sport? Fine. Be that way... But hear this: telling your possible new fuckable friend will make you less fuckable.)

Dominance. It's hot. We *want* you to be dominant! But please be discreet! A dominant woman dominates her life. She's use to being in charge of employees, money, activities, and possibly kids. Of course she wants a man who has slight more control in the relationship. By relationship law, a co-dominant relationship is the healthiest. But what do women *really* want? A man who pretends the decision-making and responsibility is 50/50, but who in reality, likes to and doesn't mind being the one in charge.

Dominance in the bedroom? If you're with a dominant woman, bondage is probably rated the lowest on her sex scale, so no worries. Fun is bed ahead! Chances are high for BDSM in the bedroom; but, whether you're a masochist or want to find out if your woman likes playing the submissive role, this is NOT a subject you want to bring up on your first couple of dates. In order for you to feel her out sexually, do it *without* talking in the bedroom, once you get there. **WARNING**: Men, asking a woman if she likes to get her ass slapped during nooky, is not a good choice. Whether she does or not, she *doesn't* want to be asked that on a first date if she's looking for a true, possible suitor.

Circle Jerk

What you shouldn't say:

"I don't have a best friend."

"Every Friday night, the guys and I play poker. No girls allowed."

What you should say:

"I go on a surf excursion every October with the guys."

"My best friend went to the same college as you!"

Dating a man who has healthy relationships with lifelong friends is a plus. Your date will want to know about your guy friends, and want to hear all about them! You never see a girl try harder to impress anyone in her life, compared to the first time she meets her new man's best friend. In her eyes, getting his stamp of approval is more important than her guy's mothers'. She knows how important his friends are because she knows how influential and valuable her own friends are. And if his are anything like her 'dream boyfriend's friends', they'll love to party, and love her too.

Did you know more men experiment with the same sex than women? Well, it's true. Telling your significant other the tale of your past homosexual experience may not necessarily be a bad thing. But if you bring it up within the first three dates, you'll send her running for the hills, leaving you in the Valley of Punaniless. So leave your circle jerk stories alone, and pretend your friends and you have never compared cock sizes.

What type of relationship does your woman want you to have with your friends? A manly one! Hopefully, you are all the same sex. If you do have that one girl in the group that hangs out with all of the guys, she should not be a threat to your woman unless she's better looking or you've hooked up in the past. So to keep things straight, make sure "your friend' knows to avoid mentioning to your new girl what happened last New Year's Eve, when the two of you woke up in some strange bed, and her panties were hanging from the ceiling fan. Just in case, you may want to pretend that she is not included in your strong group of friends. If she is brought up in conversation, make her sound as if she's an outside friend who hangs out with you guys every once in a while. Make it seem as though her presence is a nice addition every once in a while, but not a necessity. Your best buds should consist of a few guys from high school, college, or work that you get together with on a regular or not so regular basis. If this is the case, she'll love it and be more than accepting!

What a girl wants to hear is that you have a solid group of friends that you'd love her to get to know in the future. "Oh, you'd love (so-and-so)," is a great line. It insinuates that you have a friend that would get along with her, and you'd like to one day introduce them to each other. As long as you imply that she can be a part of that branch of your life, the feeling of security will set in. If the woman is included, *or at least made to feel* as if she's included, she'll have the mentality to know when to give her man space. An open invite to hanging out with your friends should always be offered. She'll feel grateful and there will be no need for jealousy to occur. She'll attend the get-togethers from time to time, but know when to give you time alone. You see, if this was a different type of woman, an open invite would be a disaster waiting to happen. She'd get used to tagging along on a regular basis, and on that one time that you don't voice an invitation, she'd freak out thinking she wasn't invited for a reason, other than the pure fact, you just need space. Luckily, your new type of woman has her own agenda, and will probably book an afternoon at the spa with her friends while you're chugging beers at the bar with yours. Having her own life, she'll appreciate her time alone with her friends and respect your time alone with yours. With this type of woman, there will be no need to ask for a night out with the guys. She's intuitive enough to know when you need it and will grant it without question.

So, as long as you share enough details to let her know that your friends and you have a strong pact, but allow visitation rights for girlfriends she'll be happy with your friendship status. Don't act as if when you and the guys get together secrets occur. Remember to be open and inviting (even if you have no intentions on having her around when you're hanging out in the man cave). She can always be uninvited after you've rated her talent in the bedroom.

Ghettoization

What you shouldn't say:

"I used to have fish. I had three of them. All goldfish. There was Cornelius, Sam and Leroy. After the first night, Sam was killed. At first, I thought it was Leroy, because-ya know....he was black! But then, the next morning, Leroy had gone belly-up! It turns out Cornelius was the mother-fucking murderer!"

"Hey! Look at that cock-asian!"

What you should say:

"I'm not racist. I just hate stupid people."

"Too many people in this world spend their time bitching and moaning, instead of actually doing something with their lives! And what I mean by that is get an education, and get a job. It's as simple as that."

"Why is a racist like a drunk? Because everything they say ends in a slur," is a great start to your debate is the Ghettoization of America. It's funny how the media has allowed minorities to dominate the United States' culture. And so be it! There are a lot of white people who take pride in their culturally eclectic music collection. And who wouldn't want to get down on the dance floor with J-Lo, sexy Enrique and Beyoncé's ass? Damn, if only Eminem were black-If investigated by the music police, some of us would come off as one of the most culturally competent people of the world!

And *Fox* news? No wait! Even better: *TBS*? Ha ha. That channel altogether is the reason why Ebonics is still **not** considered unlawful. Yes, they're ingenious for creating a station, that talks down to our society, in order to entertain those who never completed high school. And you know what?!?!?! Their ratings are insanely high, considering these are the people that keep populating our Earth and have nothing to do but sit their unemployed asses home, while watching *Tyler Perry* sitcoms. Whatever happened to *The Cosby Show*? Generations would watch that show and not even notice the pigment difference. It truly indicated that education is everything.

Believe it or not, racism is a HUGE issue in our world today. And what makes it worse is that if asked, most of us would honestly say it's not a problem anymore. These types of people have been raised in sheltered lifestyles, and have somehow, instinctively gained the insight to plead ignorance when it comes to racial issues in our society. If this is you, don't bring up your thoughts on the "laziness" of our society unless your girl has made it clear that she too, is a politically correct racist.

All in all, if you have respect for other cultures, when joke time comes around, you shouldn't be asking another name for a black, Irish midget. And if you have any sense at all, do NOT say the word "Nigger". Are you insane? Yes, it's difficult for some to make sense of why black people use it as a term of endearment, and if a white person says it they get shot in the head. But come on! Be respectful! P.S. It's ok to call them "black". It's what they are! If you start throwing around the term "African Americans", you're going to come off as trying too hard to be politically correct. And just for educational purposes, Indians (and only some) speak Hindi. *Hindu* is a religion…Jack Ass…

No matter what you think, it has been difficult for non-white races to develop a respect and live an equal lifestyle in this country. Racist comments, whether just meant for fun or for real, are wrong and offensive. No matter what your woman's background is, if she is the type of woman this book is trying to help you catch, she's not going to want to spend time with a racist. If a woman hears you referring to your maintenance men as "the spics" or you express that your Calculus professor was a chink, she's going to automatically assume you're a bigot. The first thing that is going to run through her mind is, "Oh my God. If I ever had kids with this guy they'd be such little assholes!" Racism is NOT something an intellectual woman wants passed down in her generation.

So, if you're a Saltine lover or a Douchebag Soufflé, avoid racial terminology. I'm not saying to play devil's advocate and argue, "Who's to say their way of living is wrong and our way is right?" But a respectful woman wants a respectful man. So, please douse down racial innuendos, and make it clear that you're not a fan of a specific color. You're simply a fan of intelligence.

Sexting

What you shouldn't say:

"Send me a pic."

"Why won't you answer me?"

What you should say:

"Did you get home safely?"

"Hey."

Text messaging is the way to go! Phone calls are nice *if* you AND your girl are "phone" people, but text messaging the easiest way to communicate without coming on too strong. When a woman receives a text message from the guy she's dating, it lets her know he's thinking about her, and puts a smile on her face. But if she's not responding, don't text again. If she doesn't see it, she'll respond when she does. All you need to text is a simple, "Hey". You'll hear back from her soon enough.

When communicating with your girl through text messaging, it doesn't have to be like *PONG*. It's ok to say a few things in a row, but not when you're first trying to get her attention. If she's not responding, don't text again. She'll have a much better reaction when she finally gets a chance to look at her phone to your "Hey", rather than, "Hi Hon!", "How are you?", "Why aren't you answering my texts?", "I guess you're working.", "OK! Call me when you're free!" (Please refer to the Velcro topic.)

Safe and sweet things girls want to read from their guys are as follows: a check to see if she got home safely, the planning of a second or third date, an inside joke that was already established on a past date, or a plain and simple, "Hey!" If she has time to chat it up, she'll continue the conversation.

Dirty, obnoxious texts that will make your date roll her eyes from disgust are as follows: anything sexual and any compliments (say them to her face, not her phone). Once you get to know her and have screwed around a few times, you can start the whole phone sex shit. But don't think in a million years that asking her for a nudey pic is going to turn her on. Whether it's to beat off to, show your

77

buddies the new hot tits your dating, or whatever other reason you may have, asking her to send a naked picture of herself is going to make her feel awkward, annoyed and possibly insulted. Besides, a smart girl is not going to send naked pictures of herself to someone she barely knows. (And if for some reason she sends you one, skip on down to the Joygasm topic.) Men are more visual when it comes to sex. Girls are more emotional. Asking her for a "pic" can be the worst thing you can possibly text a girl if you're trying to get her in the sack.

Careful! Your text messages reveal your English skills. If you're not a good writer, she may double guess your intelligence. She doesn't give a shit if you're from the "text generation". She expects you to speak and text proper English at all times. "A lot" is two words. Same goes for "a little". That's how it's always been, and that's how it's going to always be. Avoid all acronyms. You're a grown man! "TMOR", "B4" and "2nte?" should all be spelled out. In fact, the only usual acceptable text abbreviation is "ETA". That's because is expresses that you're a busy man, but are trying to plan ahead so you're not late for your date. Somewhere along the timeline, "LOL" somehow became conventional, but try to use some "Ha ha"s in place of your loling. Smiley faces always work as well. A person generally reacts to a smile by smiling in return. And this smile will release happy hormones, like endorphins, as well as lower stress hormones. You really can't go wrong with a smiley. Too many may make you come off as gay (pun intended), but whatever.

Velcro

What you shouldn't say:

"I think I love you."

"Call me when you wake up in the morning!"

What you should say:

"Do me a favor. Text me when you get home, so I know you're safe."

"When can I see you again?"

Let's start with *Facebook*. Within the first three dates, involving your *Facebook* pages in any way should be prohibited. *If* and *when* you talk about *Facebook*, be sure to mention that you are NOT a fan. Make sure you knock all of the friends or shall we say, acquaintances, which have no life and spend their day announcing meaningless, mediocre happenings. Don't even suggest becoming friends. It's only going to make her think her photos are now under surveillance. You know what she looks like. She's standing right in front of you! Wanting to see her *Facebook* page is what a stalker would want. And please…if she does or says something entertaining; please don't reply with a, "Oh! I like that!" accompanied by a thumbs up.

Any sign of clinginess is a sign of weakness. That in and of itself, will not make a girl want you to give her Arabian Goggles. At the same token, girls like games, but not relationship games. **If you like her let her know**! This concept is foreign to most men, because they think if they make it clear on a first date, that they'd like to book a second, it's a sign of clinginess. Absolutely not! Being direct and letting her know you like her is a gift that is well appreciated by all women. Yes, the butterflies are a good thing to have, but when you create too many questions for her to figure out, *just* to determine whether or not you're into her, the self-interrogation can be exhausting. You have to be clear that she'll be on your mind until the next time you meet, and be clear that you want a second date. Just don't go about doing this by asking her if her legs are tired.

Four letter words you should be focusing on during the first three dates: fuck, lick, kiss, date, boob, wine, dine, hard, cock, good, time and feet (for you fetishers-it's fine! Just don't talk about it!). The four letter word you should be avoiding at all costs: love. Within the first three dates, the only time you should be using the word "love" is when you're describing your feelings towards your pet. Not your mom, not your ex, and definitely not towards your date. If she trips over the curb, and laughs off her clumsiness, it's ok for you to say, "I love **it**." Why? Because you are commenting on your attraction towards an insecurity of hers. It'll make her smile and blush. But don't tell her you love an attribute of hers that is flawless. How many times do you think a guy has looked her deeply in her eyes and stated how much he loved them? Come on! EVERYONE on Earth has beautiful eyes! Could you be more unoriginal? No matter what you compliment or how you compliment, just try to stay away from the whole lovey-dovey crap.

Other things to avoid: 1) Don't ask a girl to rearrange her plans next weekend so she can go to an event with you. 2) Don't ask a girl to install a program so the two of you can video chat for free, 3) Tell her that you had plans with a friend, but are willing to uninvite them if she wants to go in their place, and 4) If it comes up that she is dating other people, don't act like you own her and if she continues to see other men it would be considered cheating. You don't *own* her! Letting your date know you are seeing other people is a dick move. If you're seeing other people, do not let her know...EVER! If she lets you in on her little secret that you're not the only one in her life, play it cool, Kid. Don't throw it back at her, and act like you don't expect anything to come from this. And again, don't let her think you're ok with it because you have a ton of women on the side as back-ups. Step up your game! It's now a competition, and you love to win, right??! So win!

Finally, use text messaging to your advantage. *Facebook*ing, instant messaging, and video chatting should not be used when wanting to communicate with your woman. Unless you are completely charismatic and do well on the phone, use the easy route. Text! Notice, how there are two "T"s in that word, and no "S". Sexting is one *quick*-ass way to send a woman running for the hills. Do not try to have sex with your woman any other way than in person within the first three dates. You have more of a chance of getting oral on the first date than getting her riled up through your dirty words early on. Texting is great, because you can keep things short and to the point. And make sure you do! If she wants to chat it up further, she'll let you know by continuing the conversation. As someone who is always accessible, it's hard to run from communication. You can pretty much bet if she's not answering your phone call, it's not because she didn't hear the phone ring. It's because she doesn't want to. As a final note, if you contact a girl two times and she doesn't respond, it's over. Two....not three....just two.

East Coast vs. West Side

What you shouldn't say:

"So, are you friends with any celebrities?"

"Oh, you're from Jersey?" (with a look of disgust)

What you should say:

"Do you surf?"

"Do prefer to ski/snowboard in Vermont or out west?"

Certainly there are similarities between the east coast and the west side. In fact, if you match up latitudes, it's quite shocking! The hippie, crunchy, organic northerners, ranging from Oregon to Vermont, are about 45 degrees north. The gays in NYC are within a few degrees of the gays in San Francisco. And according to weather.com, not only are America's finest city and the New York of the South within the same latitudinal range, they are also two of the top worst cities for traffic.

Stereotypes are there for a reason, but of course aren't always true. When you're talking about someone's homeland, they can become quite defensive if you assume they and/or their loved ones represent every stereotype assigned to their area. Not everyone from California smokes pot. And not every northerner is a bitch. Yes, they may smile and greet you as you pass them on the streets, but this is true for many people who live in high populated cities. The reason is they are surrounded by thousands of strangers everyday and are more accustomed to ignoring everyone than acting like the thought of becoming friends with everyone was a possibility.

When questioning your date on their background, you're going to want to use the knowledge you have of where they're from, which could possibly be based off stereotypes. So, use them to your advantage and ask away! Just be polite and if she's proud of where she's from, don't say anything insulting in a serious manner.

Outdoor activities are always an easy-going topic and you can mold the questions towards her if you know where she's from. This small talk can make a weak conversation into a long, yet fun discussion. Watch:

Awkward pause? If your woman is from the north (east or west side), ask if she skis or snowboards. If she does, follow-up with asking her preferred location. Share your preference and then tell a personal anecdote of the time you and your college buddies rented a cabin in Vermont and got wasted. Hungover, your friend said he'd meet you at the peak of the mountain at noon. When he got off the ski lift, he finally realized he had forgotten his snowboard at the cabin. Fucking idiot, he was!

If your woman is from the south, she is probably close enough to a beach to make the act of "beaching" more of a routine, rather than a vacationing activity. Ask her if she surfs! If so, awesome! If not, she'll tell you what she has done, and the conversation will continue. Just don't make the mistake to justify your surfing technique, if her answer is yes. She doesn't want you think that you're the next Kelly Slater, since you tried long boarding once in Waikiki. That goes for any outdoor activity. If she has done it and you *aren't good at it*, don't act like you are. Simply mention that you've tried it, followed by a pompous, "You can teach me."

Just because you don't want to judge her and focus on the stereotypes of her area, don't give her ammo, in any way, to allow her to categorize you. Example? If you're originally from Seattle, don't bore her with depressing, rainy stories of your high school years; otherwise, the woman from sunny St. Petersburg, Florida staring at you from the opposite side of the table is going to think that you were suicidal in high school, and spend the rest of the date wondering is suicide is hereditary.

Your Fish Seems Confused!

What you shouldn't say:

"The Bible is a crock of shit."

"And then I say to myself, 'What Would Jesus Do?'"

What you should say:

"I'm spiritual, but I wouldn't say religious."

"I'm a CEO, you know, a fair-weather Christian. I go to church on Christmas and Easter only."

Yelling "Oh my God!" might be forgivable when one's yelling it out in the bedroom. Perhaps if you're trying to cross the street with your date in the city, and a taxi driver almost takes your arm off, it might be acceptable as well. But using the Lord's name in vain can be quite offensive to some people. Here's a quick hint: avoid the term "Jesus Christ!" It automatically shows you don't have a strong faith. Remember, religion is sacred to people. For some, it might be the most important thing in their lives. Others? Might not give a shit! And for all of the people in between, well…you'll have to learn through trial and error.

OR…..YOU CAN JUST **NOT** BRING IT UP!!!!

But if you want to go ahead and talk about religious views, so be it. But religion is like politics. You don't necessarily look stupid if you know nothing about it, but you can come off as heartless. As long as the two of you are respectful, you should be fine. Everyone has their own opinions, so recognize that accordance is never going to happen. This isn't math. There is not one right answer, and people feel strongly about their God(s), or lack thereof. So, no matter what you do, don't act like her views are in any way wrong. What that means is don't sigh after she's explained her Baptist beliefs and reply, "Well…everyone has their own opinion." Instead, nicely comment on the Baptist religion. It's ok to let her that know you don't know much about the religion, but don't in any way let her think that there's no way in hell you'd ever share any beliefs with her.

If your conversation goes from personal to philosophical, watch for cues to see if she's falling asleep. If her head falls off her hand, hits the soup bowl, that's your cue! SHUT IT! If you come off as if you're currently studying religious views, it's a complete turn-off. She'll be wondering if you're confused, and get angry because your explanation of how you're a Christian AND believe in evolution, but still find ways to incorporate Buddhist rituals is making her want to slit her wrists.

The top religions of our country include Christianity, Judaism, Islam, Buddhism, Non-religion/Secularism, Atheism, and so on. There are many choices. Back to the *Smart-Ass* topic, once you find out your woman's sense of humor and faith background, there is a slight chance you can make some jokes. The whole priest, rabbi and lawyer/monk-whatever jokes are hilarious. But only say them in context. If there's a pause during your date, don't break in with, "So, do you want to hear a joke?" That will not make her want you. It will just make her thankful that you found a way to break the silence barrier. As for Scientology jokes, bring 'em on! We're sorry, but what Tom Cruise has done to the religion of Scientology, is exactly what *MTV's Jersey Shore* has done for Italians in New Jersey. They've created a disgrace of their culture. If you are a Scientologist-or much worse, an Italian Scientologist from New Jersey, *don't* tell your woman! In her eyes, the reason why you are taking religion seriously is because you are trying to *find* yourself. If you start talking about your level, she won't even waste her time excusing herself to go to the bathroom, call her friend and plan an emergency phone call five minutes later. She'll just get up and leave.

If you are a religious man yourself, good for you! But depending on your involvement with your religious sanctuary might be a deal breaker. If you are really involved, and she's not, stop talking about it. Please don't bore her with the nitty-gritty details of your beliefs. When it comes to religion, it's easier to disagree with someone else's views that agree with them. So don't give her any reason to get pissed off at what you believe in. You'll look like a religious freak. How do you do this? Don't go into detail about your faith! And if you're a born again Christian, and are waiting until marriage....why the hell did you even buy this book!?!! (This book has not been made to help you get married within three dates) That girl will run! She'll run as if the winner of the race gets to make out with Ryan Reynolds! (And that's going to be fucking fast!)

Don't believe in God? Fine! That's your choice; but, a harsh one to a woman who wants her kids to grow up with some kind of faith. Generations today don't favor going to church, temple or mosque like they did decades and even centuries ago. It's a new age. A lazy age... What a woman really wants is a man who grew up in a Catholic family, but as an adult, firmly disagrees with their values. It's the same as politics. What a woman really wants is a man who grew up in a conservative, republican family, but who has veered off because of his wild and crazy college nights! Why? Because those values are still infused and are a part of him. And one day, if the two of you ever have kids, you'll make sure that faith is a priority for your kids...until they go off to college. (It's one vicious religious circle!) This gives a calming sense to the woman who has too, veered off from the religion she once lived by. It's not forgotten, but it's still extremely important to her that it remains true to her and her family.

Again, don't go into too much detail, no matter how religious you are. This isn't a prayer group, it's a first date. And your goal is to get laid, not explain the Theravada, the Qur'an, or give excuses why you feel as though you should be allowed into heaven. If you end up giving her a lesson on Pacifism, Mohammad, or Mr. Smith, in her head, she'll be singing, "Dum, dum, dum, dum, dum!"

Obama or Osama?

What you shouldn't say:

"Do you vote?"

"Who's your favorite President and why?"

What you should say:

"My parents are republicans."

"I don't watch the news. I watch Jon Stewart...Just kidding. I keep in tune."

As Winston Churchill would say, if you are 20 years old and you aren't a liberal you have no heart, and if your 50 years old and you are a liberal, you have no brain. As successful women would say, if you are 20 years old and you are a liberal, you are unemployed. If you are 50 years old and you are a liberal, you are unemployed. Keep this in mind, when discussing your political parties.

Politics is possibly the most notorious subject NOT to bring up on one of the first few dates. Honestly, if you really find it necessary to talk about the so-called "recession", more like depression, that is affecting our country, go ahead. But don't be bringing it up just to use it as an excuse for your unemployment. It's not necessarily like a discussion on the overall failures of the presidential candidates is a bad idea, but it's easy to criticize. So, don't go overboard. -Not like you could do any better in their position, so don't go acting like if you were king, the world would be a better place. This is a quick way to look like an idiot in front of your woman.

Again, it's not that politics are always a bad subject to discuss when you first meet someone. It *can* be filled with passion and enthusiasm! Unfortunately, 95% of the time, it will be filled with boredom and monotone non sequiturs. Feel her out for her urge to talk about politics. A good way to tell if she might be interested to opine about politics, is to evaluate what she does. Does she work for the government? Education? A political party? If her career is highly influenced by politics, she should be in the loop. Whether or not she wants to talk about it is a different story. Perhaps she is sick of the discussion. Perhaps she's used to men automatically tailoring their conversations to politics because they think she is interested. Or maybe she's passionate and likes a good political debate over a nice glass of wine! Then again, you could always come right out and say it. "Do you like politics?"

Keep in mind, if the woman does have a career in politics and you do not, you should shy away from discussing them unless you are 100% sure you can hold your own. This is probably why she is still single. Because every guy she dates starts out with trying to impress her, only to reveal his shallow-minded imbecility. If you MUST discuss, bring up specific things that you know details about. Don't try to summarize your views on America's progressive policies. Try commenting on Silvio Berlusconi and his 'bunga bunga' parties, and BAM! You've just made her laugh and at the same time, come off as someone who knows their international affairs! (One thing that Prime Minister isn't for sure is an orgy-fucking fascist!)

If you're with a woman that is above your average standards, then let's just assume that she knows her shit. But, let's be honest, the real reason why people don't like to talk politics at the table is because it's a quick way to make someone feel stupid. You might as well bring out an IQ test and tell them that they have two hours to complete the following. You see, one doesn't need a degree to know what's going on in the world today. Schools don't even teach that shit anyway! The only thing someone needs is a TV or the internet. And who the fuck doesn't have that?!?! It's real easy to know if someone's an idiot if they don't know what's going on in the world today. The problem is, not many people do! And if you have a hard working female on the other end of the bar, blankly staring at you when you ask for her thoughts on the vice-president (who she can't even name), inferiority is going to reveal itself. Yeah, perhaps her mistake of mixing up Osama and Obama was purely a blonde moment, but then again someone on that date is going to be judging her for her error. And whether it's you or her, chances are she's going to want to get the hell out of there, due to pure embarrassment.

Jammin'

What you shouldn't say:

"I love Broadway tunes."

"Listen to this song…it really makes you think."

What you should say:

"What's your favorite song?"

"If you could have a theme song every time you walked into a room, what would it be?"

So, "What music do you listen to," is a pointless question. Who the fuck cares? Is it going to make any more of a difference of how you look at her? Knowing what type of music each of you listens to isn't going to change the way you feel about each other. Taking this into account, the subject of music is considered nothing but **small talk**.

Unless you or your girl work in the music industry or enjoy going to concerts, music is no more special to either of you than it is to the rest of society. Remember, people are passionate about music. Music brings out emotion. Whether you're singing at a karaoke bar, rockin' out to the radio in your car, or screaming your lungs out in the shower, you are releasing endorphins throughout your body. It is a healing process, which is why certain songs make people emotional. So, don't tease her too much about her love for Michael Jackson. She may take offense to it. Granted, if she's moon walking to the bathroom, she's most likely waiting for a wise crack.

If the girl is a concert fanatic-BINGO! Conversation has just found an inlet. Ask her what concerts she's been to. Ever been back stage? How many Dave Matthew's concerts has she been to? If she's enjoying herself while telling you these stories, let her entertain herself. And if you have a couple of musical tales of your own, go ahead and jump in.

For those of you boys who are still practicing with your garage band, it may not be smart to bring that up. Back in high school, it was cute. You had a chance! But let's face it. You and your band are going nowhere, so if you think you still have a chance of signing with a record label-keep it to yourself. She'll instantly label you as "loser" and want to walk away. If your relationship continues after the third date and you want to keep her around, it's best to say you go out every Wednesday night and "jam with the guys". Even if we are serious about a guy, we don't want to know about his little band project. It's embarrassing to tell our friends that our 32-year old boyfriend is still in a garage band.

Just keep in mind that the subject of music should not mean anything more than what the weather looks like tomorrow. Small talk is simply a filler in conversation. Don't talk her ear off about Pantera. Don't try to convince her that she hasn't listened to enough rap to recognize the true passion behind the words. And finally, if she's not a fan of jazz, don't tap and scat repetitively throughout the night. If the subject comes up, don't be judgmental, and if she's smart, she won't be either.

Fumble

What you shouldn't say:

"Every Sunday I watch football all day long. I can't live without it."

"Let me guess. Your favorite sport is figure skating?"

What you should say:

"What's your favorite sport?"

"I have season tickets to the (name your team)."

Will your date be a girl who is obsessed with sports? Perhaps. But let's be honest, sports were created to help men practice their communication skills. It helps them socialize with each other. Without sports, occasions like dinner parties and family events wouldn't exist! We wouldn't be able to bring you anywhere! You'd just sit there in the corner, moping with your sappy face. To compromise, we allow sports to exist on the face of this planet, and allow them to entertain you, as they so very well do.

Men love competition! It's why you bought this book. You're trying to learn how to bang the hottest woman out of all of your friends. So, when you bring her out and people look her up and down, you can think to yourself, *"that's right bitches! She's mine!"* Notice how when you take a couple and rate their looks, the girl is *always* hotter? That is because the guy works harder to attract his sexy mate. Claiming that sweet-ass builds his reputation, as well as his ego. So, she'll let you compete, and if you pass all of the rules, you'll get your victory. Admit it! You've fucked a hot girl before and sang the only non-gay Queen song ever made in your head, "We Are the Champions".

Men who are obsessed with sports: use your brain. We don't care how much of a sports fanatic your woman is, she doesn't want to go home after a night out and remember nothing but stats. A good fumble is when you're fumbling around the room the next morning looking for your pants. A bad fumble is when you're fumbling around for topics to discuss other than Randy Moss' most notorious catch. So, recept your shit, and use sports topics to your advantage. Just be sure to not overdo it and if you see her yawning while you're discussing the relationship between Joe Montana and Jerry Rice, know when to stop.

Ask her, "So, what's your favorite sport?" Don't ask if she *likes* sports. For God's sake! It's the twenty-first century! Everything's considered a sport, these days! Whether it's ice-skating or fucking poker, she'll be able to pick one to discuss. And when discussing your favorite hometown teams, it correlates you to where you're from! So if you're routing for Philly teams, expect her to associate you with trash…especially if she's a fan of dogs.

If her answer to your sports questions is, "I really don't like sports," then tell her whatever she wants to hear to get her in bed with you. It really won't matter, because you know as well as anyone, if sports play no part in her life, she's not going to make it to round four. When she's mentioning Ray Finkle's laces, you know she's clueless. So, shut up about the finals for the time being and save it for the next girl who has an interest.

As long as this girl has had masculine men play a role in her life (and if she's on top of her game, the answer to that is yes), she should be able to hold her own when it comes to discussing a sport or two. The question is: what happens when you date a girl that knows more about sports than you do? It's embarrassing enough if your chick can throw a better spiral than your meek, little arm can muster. And if that's true for you, go to the fucking gym, little man. If you start to realize that her knowledge on last weekend's *PTI* show surpasses yours, pardon *this* interruption-but you're a pussy! Take a pass-to another topic! Meeting a guy who knows little to nothing about sports is not a turn-on. Now, if your forte is football, but you know shit about her favorite sport, hockey, follow the notorious advice: stick to what you know. Let her chat a little about her favorite *Lightning* player, who was the star Canadian for Texas and is upsettingly now a *Ranger*. Then, switch it back to your sport or at least one that you can converse about. Is it hot to date a girl who knows about sports? Most men say yes. But if you ask a girl who knows a lot about sports if it's hot to date a guy who isn't a sports fan, her answer will always remain the same. No.

Noodling

What you shouldn't say:

"Git-R-Done!"

"The movie *Varsity Blues* was filmed in my hometown!"

What you should say:

"I grew up in the south, but I went to college up north. I'm very thankful for that."

"The school system down south sucks."

Here's a clue: if you're mamma named you Billy Bob, Billy Joe or Billy Ray. **Change it!** No woman in her educated, right mind wants to date you. And if your family or friends nicknamed you Junior or Bubba, keep them away from your woman until she's slept with you, fallen in love with you and married you. Otherwise, she won't come back now, Yeehaw! Whether it's your real name or a screen name, southern labels are deal breakers.

Speaking of names, if your dog is named something redneck like, "Harley"-ignore that too. If she asks, "What's his name?" Just respond with the classic, "I don't know! He never told me!" And move onto the next subject.

The term redneck is a derogatory name that was originally given to poor, white men that worked on farms. Their necks were frequently red from the sun's rays. Happily, the idiotic farmers proudly embraced the label and eventually in the twentieth century, the union workers of the United Mine Workers of America (UMW) used red bandannas around their neck as a symbol of their solidarity. The color red can also symbolize the blood spilled on Blair Mountain, or even the Rebel Flag; which by the way, if you own one of these; you're not necessarily going to be assumed to be a racist. But you will be assumed to be an idiot, who is proud of your southern heritage and is tightly holding on to a horrible piece of history for some insane reason. LET GO OF THE PAST! IT'S NOT EVEN YOURS!

If you're a redneck, basically everyone's out of your league! Especially, the girl who you are trying to lay. The number one stereotype for rednecks is stupidity. The challenge here is to neglect that stereotype and provide reasons why your woman should not associate you with the true southern trash. So if you've been called a "redneck" in your lifetime, avoid the following terms/topics: Monster Trucks, *Nascar, Larry the Cable Guy,* Catfish, chewing tobacco, your hometown in one of the twin states, favorite straw hat, or the trough. Your negative epithet will not get you laid...by a human of course. 27% of people who grew up on a farm had their first sexual experience with a farm animal, you know. Do you really want her wondering the details of *your* first time? Perhaps it was with the bull of whose balls are hanging off the tail end of your pick-up truck. Get it, men? Avoid all southern terminology.

As for southern music? Yes! It is true that many women are a fan of the country twang! These women find the music relevant, emotional and sexy. But before you start booking concert tickets to Keith Urban, be sure to ask her what type of music she likes. If her answer is, "Anything but country and rap," don't let her know that every Saturday night you line dance. If she says she appreciates country, maybe you could sing her a little tune. That is, if you're not tone deaf. If she is a fan, use it to your advantage. Music can be very romantic...even if it's singing about cardboard boxes and Chevys.

On a positive note, you'll never hear a woman say she doesn't like a man with an accent. And a good southern accent indicates good, southern charm. And yes, it often happens where the most absolute, red-neck farm boy is dating the hottest ass in bum-fuck nowhere. Why? Because she's attracted to this rugged and handy gentleman. Unfortunately, this negative predisposition for people to stereotype southerners as dumbasses does exist! So, if you're an idiot from Mississippi, asking your date the riddle, "What has four eyes?" she'll eventually correlate your south drawl with a low IQ. Just try your best to show her some signs of intelligence.

Finally, if you're a fan of good southern cookin', you may be the only one. If you're girl is from up north, don't suggest a good southern restaurant or hearty BBQ. If you're really excited about the idea, she might just agree out of politeness. The truth is, not many northerners have a craving for fried chicken, mashed potatoes and gravy. In fact, if your girl has any sort of figure, it's because she's probably spent her entire life avoiding southern cooking at all costs. Finally, one of the two types of food a woman wants to steer clear of on the first few dates is BBQ. (In case you're wondering, the other is crab legs.) Yes, she might find it delicious, but the type of sauce that she wants her new man to watch her slop all over her face and lick off her fingers with a "yumming" moan, is not barbeque.

Deep as a Puddle

What you shouldn't say:

"It really makes you think."

"I'm a part of a think tank."

What you should say:

"I don't like wasting my time."

"I don't give much thought to things that don't matter."

Do you remember having free time back in high school? You used to lock your door, turn on your cassette player, lie on your bed and **think**. Nowadays, things are a tad different. *If* you have free alone time, you *do* go lock your door and turn your mp3 player on, but you don't waste time thinking. You spend those few, precious moments jacking off!

Who the hell has time to *think* these days? If you do, you need to get a job. Sure! Thinking hard is good. But if you're going to get all philosophical on us, stand back! We just might puke.

Owning up to taking part in emo music, skinny jeans, or chain emails will not get you laid. Please get this down pat-we don't want an emotional man, who likes mulling over thoughts and feelings. If you're a psychologist, you have an excuse: it's your job. But please don't try to over analyze our thoughts and/or actions.

Religion is one thing. It's normal for people to spend a large portion of their lives contemplating the "unknown". But, Philosophy? No matter how good your logic defending the importance of epistemology over metaphysics is, the one you are trying to court will probably think it's a waste of time. And if so, she's not the type of woman that wants to be with a man who is going to overload her brain every evening with thoughts on thoughts. Sure, philosophical topics may be interesting. We all took a class or two in college, and back then philosophy plus pot equaled fun! But chances are the woman you're with is a realist. She is in search of a man who has a similar outlook on life, and who has answers. If you're still searching for yourself, get lost. A man, who is searching for life's answers, is a man we're not interested in.

For instance, the following is a 'no-no': Don't get drunk, and tell your date that you have been working on a theory for years, and plan on changing the world. (And if you do, and she asks for more information, know it's not because she's actually interested, but because she now thinks you're a tool, and wants the material so she can laugh it off with her friends later.) Don't continue to tell her that the name of your theory is "The Theory of It All". (Seriously?!?) And please don't continue to say that you plan on getting rid of religion and politics in the world, because they aren't needed for us to live in today's century. (Really...*is that all*?) And don't further explain that you intend on changing society's mind by paying people to forget about their Gods and leaders. (Yes, true story. And the most ironic part about it was, is he had just finished explaining how he had been unemployed for the past six months.) The girl's response: "Really...and how do you plan on getting the funding to pay these people enough money to ignore and forget about the most important thing they believe in?" <Pause> "You know what? I can see it happening! Because it's not going to be hard for me to ignore and forget you! And I'll be doing it free of charge!" Needless to say, he did not get laid.

Conspiracy theories, on the other hand, are tons of fun to mention! Smart people usually love riddles, jokes or entertaining narratives that are tricky to figure out. A conspiracy theory is a wild assumption thought up by highly intellectual individuals; therefore, bring it on! If you know anything about one or two, they'll at least keep your woman's interest.

If you're reading your woman and you think she would like a man with a calm and thoughtful disposition, tell her you do yoga. You may think yoga is a sissy activity, but you'll never meet a woman who doesn't like yoga. And having a yoga partner is always a fun thing. Knowing that you are interested in the relaxing, meditative behavior will be a nice thought for her. For one, it could possibly be an activity you do together as a couple, and two, you're probably very sensual in bed.

What if you're an introvert who takes pride in his thinking sessions? That's fine! Do it on your own time though. In the dating scene come out of your shell, little clam! Imagination is a miraculous tool to have as an adult. And if you possess a powerful one, it will help you maintain romance in the relationship. But discussing your imaginative thoughts on life can be dangerous in the beginning. To play it safe, it's best to hide every ounce of your naivety, and discuss pertinent matters. Follow through with good conversation and save your pensive persona for another time.

I Work Out!

What you shouldn't say:

"My muscles are so cut today! I don't know why…I didn't even work out!"

"You know the more you use a muscle, the bigger it gets. That's why I have such big feet-if you know what I mean!!!"

What you should say:

"Do you workout?"

"Do you do yoga?"

The cock is **NOT** a muscle, Jack Ass. It stops growing when you're in your early twenties, so if you're not at the height and width that you had hoped to reach, tough shit. Learn to live with what you have.

You know that look a girl gives you with wide eyes, tall arched eyebrows, the least bit of a smile and a tiny nod? No? Brag to her about how much you bench-press, and then you'll know what we're talking about. Here's another thing you must know: men stare at tits, as if they were little leprechauns and they see not only one, but *two* pots of gold at the end of the rainbow! Women do not do the same to men's pecs. They do to arms, soccer thighs and abs bumpy enough for them to do their laundry on. But pecs? Not so much. Now that you know this, please refrain from letting your woman in on your little secret that you can flex your pecs one at a time. Ew.

For all of you losers who like taking pictures of your top half with your camera phone in your bathroom and posting them on the internet. My God! And you wonder why girls don't respond to your inquiries on your dating website. First of all, half of your bodies *aren't* that attractive! Second of all, you seem REALLY into yourself. Thirdly, that act is a sign of you either being insecure or stupid. Please note, if you have a good body, you don't have to flaunt it OR talk about it. Girls have eyes! And even if you were dating a blind chick, her friends have eyes. And they'll be bound to tell her that the guy she's dating has a body of a champ.

For those of you who do have a great body, let's now talk about why you shouldn't discuss working out to your new woman. The majority of women in this country have a huge insecurity issue with their bodies. Even if they have rockin' bodies, they have a way of finding the flaws and focusing in on them. If you sit there for half of the date and tell her how important being fit is to you, and how you'd like to find someone to have the same mindset, she may doubt a future with you. Being in a relationship with a guy who has a better body is hard enough. Being in a relationship with a guy who is constantly commenting on how important working out is annoying, and eventually might become insulting. Not to mention this extreme question she'll be thinking about: will you like her when she's fat with your child? And if you're really coming off as a meathead, no matter how sweet you are to her, she'll doubt you'll follow through with a relationship with a chubby, pregnant woman. It sounds crazy, we know. But no matter how secure your woman seems, body image is a different deal.

Speaking of insecurities…it's very easy for a woman to detect your own insecurity with your own body. Don't continuously give excuses on why you haven't been to the gym lately. Whether work has been crazy, you've been sick for a few weeks, or you've been partying it up too much, it's not an excuse a woman wants to hear. Either work out or don't! But don't sit there telling her *why* you haven't been. It's just not sexy.

So remember, Muscle Man. If you're accustomed to drinking *Muscle Milk*, don't ask your woman if she wants to feel your biceps. She can see what your workout ethic is like, and it's either going to intimidate her or turn her on. Are you a personal trainer? It's ok to mention it, but don't focus the conversation on your work. Just shut up about it and don't interrogate her regarding her exercise schedule. Most importantly, let her know that you think she's hot!

Zumanity

What you shouldn't say:

"I have 32 tattoos. I love body art."

"Oh, come on! How can you say that porn is *not* art?!?"

What you should say:

"I haven't been to a museum in a while. Want to go to one next weekend?"

"I wouldn't say I'm culturally incompetent, but I'm really not that into art."

Talking your woman's ear off about the Chilean artist, Alexander Sutulov, is going to make her drown your voice out as if she was watching a Charlie Brown movie. The chances that she wants to have an in-depth talk about his digital generated visuals are slim to none. Yes, the word "Chilean" is fun to say, but unless this woman has his work hanging in her house or is an Art Curator, she probably has no clue who the fuck you're talking about. Please don't try to persuade her that her new hobby should be collecting art. We're being honest, here. It's kind of gay. If she's not artsy now, she's not going to be open to becoming artsy. Plain and simple. If she's like the average American, she's not interested in becoming an art inspector. She's happy with her simple-minded job as an art respecter.

Now that you know how not to bore the shit out of her with your impeccable attention to art deco details, let's discuss ways you can use art to your advantage!

First of all, here's a quiz:

If she is a fan of art and wants to talk about it, what do you do?

...

Damn it! Haven't you learned anything from this book?!!!? YOU LISTEN! LISTEN AND SMILE! And don't forget the frequent nodding. No matter how little you know about art, you should have somewhat of a nodding acquaintance with the subject matter, so use it!

Let's move on...If you discuss things that she is passionate about during your first date, in between the first and second, you can investigate artists you think she'd like! For instance, if your woman is very passionate about Hawaii, during the second date, you can mention, "You know I was thinking...have you ever seen the work of Scott Hanson? He's this amazing sculptor from Hawaii. His work is incredible. My favorite piece is the 'Silver Seas'." She'll probably answer with a simple, "No." But you can bet your slick ass she'll GTS when she gets home, which will make her think of you when she's having her alone time...which will make her want you. It's a great move, because you're bringing up something she mentioned from the first date, letting her know that you thought about her on your off time, are a good listener, AND make her think that you are actually interested in what she has to say. Just don't do it to some dumb artist everyone knows. If your woman works with babies, don't ask her if she's ever seen Anne Geddes' work. Everyone's seen that shit.

As for trips to the museum? Great dates! Even if one doesn't like art, they'll have fun, and it strikes up obscure conversation you wouldn't normally be able to bring up on a date without sounding like a creeper. And if you live near any major city, they probably have a sex museum. (It's becoming the new thing.) You want to get fucked? Take your woman to see a *Cirque de Soleil* show. And not just any one, take her to see *Zumanity*. Another artsy visual that will in some way get her in a fucking mood is the messed up movie, *Short Bus*. Why people want to fuck when they see these odd shows is beyond our train of thought. But if you can somehow come up with an excuse to watch something sexual ***that isn't porn***, you're bound to get laid. Just make sure you make the suggestion slyly. Cause if you invite your woman back to your house and pop in *Short Bus* out of nowhere, there's a slight chance she might call the cops in fear that you're about to ass rape her.

Smart-Ass

What you shouldn't say:

"Spank you."

"Knock, knock..."

What you should say:

When you first meet/see her: "Damn. I told the agency to send me an Asian."

"So, I broke into this church at 2am."

A mother's advice: You will want to find a man that treats you well, loves you a little more than you love them, and makes you laugh!

The most impressive type of humor a man can have is wit. It's impressionable, intellectual, and clever-all wrapped into one devastatingly, attractive package. This package intrigues a woman, because it keeps her on her feet, as well as keeps her smiling! If a guy is described as witty, it makes one automatically assume that he is extremely bright. So, wit up some smart-ass comments and if you see an overload of pearly whites (no pun intended), you'll know you're doing a good job.

Perhaps wit doesn't come easily, and instead you are a master of is satire parody. Are you a frequent viewer of *The Simpsons* and *Family Guy*? If so, you better hope she is too. If she has a good sense of humor too, chances are she's somewhat of a fan. But don't go pulling one-liners if you realize she's not an admirer of the show. And that, you may figure out quickly. Keep in mind, just because you're good at remembering lines from popular media productions, doesn't mean you're funny. It means you're good at stealing other people's material. So keep your plagiarism to a minimum. The positive thing about satire parody is that it's fucking funny! Most modern day comedians excel at this type of humor. You know when you're at a comedy club and you hear cries from the audience saying, "It's *so* true!", -that's satire parody. It's the exaggeration of reality. And depending on how dirty you get, your satire approach may fall into the world of fratism. Tucker Max style. If she likes it, you're golden. But don't be in a rush to get dirty. Wade her into your muddy puddle. If she's egging for a dip, spit it out! This type of humor can have you and her rolling in the hay.

Speaking of rolling in the hay, let's roll onto the next type of "funny" you can be. Spontaneity is priceless; although, it can be tricky. When something unexpected happens, if you're talented at whipping out a punch line, go for it! For example, a short bum walks up to the two of you on the street and is being obnoxious, begging for money. The two of you forcefully try to keep walking while paying no attention to his antics. Finally, he jumps in front of you and completely blocks your way, "Come on, man! I just got pick pocketed!" You look down at him and rudely say, "Wow. How could someone stoop so low?" -and gently guide your woman past him. Improvise away!

For all of you Jeremy Piven wannabes, tendentious humor can work to an extent. Your woman should be able to handle a hit or two, and if she has a true blonde moment, she'll definitely want a guy that's going to call her out on her shit. That type of guy challenges her. And challenges are enticing!

As for the po-faced man who consistently repeats his jokes because he's memorized a handful by word playing, please refrain from, "That's what she said," and other overly annoying phrases.

Slap shots are hot, but slapsticking is not. Class clowns were funny in school because they distracted us from something boring. Constant overbearing, attention-hogging, so-called "comedy" is not how you impress a girl on the first few dates. And if you're an aspiring comedian? Fade yourself. You're not famous yet, which means there are still some nooks and crannies that need to be worked on. It doesn't matter if you've done stand-up comedy in Times Square. Anyone who has guts can book one of those gigs. Just keep in mind, if you overdo yourself, she'll start doing the wide, eye rolling of the eyes.

Finally, for all of the Boring Barrys out there, if you can't muster up the funnies, don't stress-cause it'll show!!! If it doesn't come naturally, you better pray you're a good story teller! And believe it or not, a good anecdote is a perfect way to break the conversational ice on a date! So good luck!

A Woman's Best Friend

What you shouldn't say:

"I don't like dogs."

"In September I went on a hunting trip with my brothers."

What you should say:

"I love animals."

"When I was younger, I wanted to be a vet."

Just like a mother wouldn't date a man that didn't like kids, a woman who loves her pet does not want to be with a man that doesn't. Pet owners who live alone become very attached to their mini roommates. And during certain times of a woman's biological clock, the feeling and need of attachment becomes extremely strong. If she is without a man or child, who do you think is going to be the victim? Her four-legged friend, of course!

If she does have an oddball friend, such as a snake, frog or fish, it's not the same. They're cold-blooded. But jokingly calling her canine or feline friend a bitch or a pussy will get her to end the date faster than a shit after a Taco Bell visit. Just stay away from insulting any of her little friends.

Cat vs. dog. Cats are known to be independent, self-assured and aloof. Dogs are known to be social, loyal and affectionate. Plain and simple: a dog owner is more likely to become dependent on their pet than a cat owner because of the social bond between the two species. If you are a cat man and she owns a dog that doesn't like cats, make it known that you love dogs too, and don't act like your cat is indispensable.

Learn to like THAT dog. You may not like every dog, but you have to find a way to like this one. Do not show any disdain for her dog, because if you do, she will sadly throw you aside. Guys will come and go, but a girl who's in love with her dog isn't going to get rid of it. She knows this early on, and will not get serious with any guy who would ask her to eventually make a choice. She fears that if she falls hard for him, she'd pick him and resentment would just grow from there.

What can you say to help her realize that you're interested in joining the muskinettes? Suggest activities that involve the third wheel (you). The second date is a great time to go for a walk or visit the park. "Bring the dog!" A woman wants a man that will offer to help and involve the animal in their relationship. Remember, a healthy and happy pet has a healthy and happy owner. Make her think you'll take part in the parenting position.

Maybe your woman is not a dog girl. If so, fine! You can deal with that! Perhaps she plays for the other side of the field. If she's a cat lover, avoid "cat lady" jokes. Learn to listen, and learn to act…interested. As Demetri Martin would say, "You're going to get to a point where you don't give a shit about how intuitive her cat is." If you actually get to that point, make sure you don't show it. If she's truly talking your ear off about her furry friend, it is obviously important to her, so make a note. Pretend to love it too!

Finally, depending on how much of an animal lover she truly is, avoid letting her know you take an interest in hunting. What the hell gives you the right to take a life from an innocent, little creature? Seriously! What kind of person ARE YOU!?!? Sure, since the brink of time, women have been attracted to strong men, who can hunt and gather food for us. We still are! Do you think we *like* going grocery shopping? Grab your credit card and pick up some dinner yourself! But truthfully, there is a stronger force that exists today! Her name is Sarah McLachlan. And there's no way your excuse for ending something's life is going to come off as acceptable when Sarah keeps doing those damn *ASPCA* commercials!

Whiskey Dick

What you shouldn't say:

"Let's get wasted!"

"I'm an alcoholic."

What you should say:

"Would you like another round? It's up to you."

"Want to go for a walk?"

Do you know what a rubber hose without water running through it feels like? So do we, and it's **NOT** attractive. Unfortunately, sometimes when a man drinks too much it can have an adverse reaction. And when we want sex, we *want* your attention, as well as your dick's attention! (Standing at attention, that is.) So please keep in mind that when you consume too much alcohol it can lead to a sloppy, disappointing ending, which will in turn not get you laid.

If it weren't for alcohol, you or your date would probably not exist, so cheers to the prohibition days being over! Chances are you and your date are doing something that involves alcohol, whether it's going to a bar/restaurant, playing pool, bowling, going to a comedy club, or hanging out at the beach. Excellent! Have fun! It's no secret that alcohol plays a large role in dating. Tipsiness is encouraged, but don't offer to drive if you plan on having a few too many, and don't encourage shloshiness.

Yes, it's true that alcohol can help make a date more soothing. It can also make it much more fun! But, there is a point where the alcohol consumption can start counteracting the pleasurable evening. Obviously, if you or your date drinks too much, a bad situation may occur. Forget the fact that your dick will most likely malfunction, chances are if either of you get wrecked, a future date reserved for fucking will not be set. Yes, you might get her to spend the night, but this book has been written to help you get laid without giving your girl Ruffies. There are other ways, men!

Assuming that you're smart enough to know that a girl wants a man who can control his alcohol intake, as well as sidetrack her if she's drinking too much, we'll move on to some dialogue tips about alcohol you'll want to remember.

If your girl likes to drink, she'll want to know that a) you like to drink, b) you drink often, but have it under control, and c) you don't mind if she drinks. Almost everyone has had at least one bad experience with alcohol. At *least* one! Whether your girl was the drunken mess one night or someone else was, she is well aware that alcohol is *NOT* fun unless it's in a safe environment and under control. A safe way to divulge your love for alcohol is to watch and listen to her talk about how many bottles of wine her and her roommates routinely down in one dinner. If she says she doesn't drink much, have a beer or two and move on to the next activity of the night. If she utters that she's still hung over from the fourteen keg stands she did last night, don't sweat it, and chug on!

The word you want to avoid, *always and forever*, is "alcoholic". I don't care if you want to mention you're an alcoholic in a joking matter. Steer clear of *Nike*'s slogan and just *don't* do it. The second she thinks you may have an alcohol problem; she'll be creating reasons in her head why it's not going to work. These reasons might not even be real, but like STIs, females have been known to avoid men with drug and alcohol problems. And to be honest, if a girl finds out you have an alcohol problem, the next thought that will float into her head will be the question of abuse. So if you're dependent on liquor, pull yourself together and don't show it.

On a side note: **GET HELP!**

If you are an alcoholic in recovery, good luck! Not many women who enjoy drinking will be looking for a relationship with a man that doesn't drink. It's not that she doesn't like or respect you. It's the fact that she wants to be with a man who will tolerate her drinking, and drink with her, which will allow her validate her own drinking. Even if you're completely open and ok with hanging out at bars, it will be difficult for you to convince a woman to date you. As for all of you AA-Graduates out there, take your date somewhere that doesn't involve drinking. Have her fall first, and then tell her later. Your chances of catching her will be higher.

Finally, notice how it is mentioned above that a girl wants a man who can sidetrack her if she's had too much to drink. Observe her tolerance. If she's had a few too many and starts slurring her words as if she's had too many Valium, suggest an activity that does not involve drinking. A nice walk on a scenic route is always romantic! You could also tell her you're starving, and order some food. Even if she claims she's not hungry, her sloppiness will probably pursue, and she won't think twice about stealing food off your plate and scarffing more crap down her throat. Whatever you do, *DON'T* advise her to stop drinking. The question, "Don't you think you've had enough?" is not something a woman wants to hear from a guy she's trying to impress. It will embarrass her and that alone will probably screw up your chances of getting a second date. Plus, if you're unlucky enough to have her be an angry drunk, a raging bitch might make an appearance. Your best choice is to stick to pretending that she's in complete control and take a detour to a place that is a dry location.

Around the World-And Back Again

What you shouldn't say:

"I don't like taking extravagant vacations. I'd much rather go camping in the woods with Sam (the dog)."

"It's just too expensive to travel, these days."

What you should say:

"I love to travel!"

"This upcoming (list a month within the next six months) I'll be traveling to (list an exotic location on a different continent)."

Are you a world-wide traveler or a vacationer? There's a major difference between the two. Women admire world-wide travelers. They're much more experienced, intellectual, and come from money!! A vacationer simply uses the facilities of a higher end hotel, in an exotic setting, and spends their money and time drinking and playing. A girl doesn't care much for a vacationer... *Unless*, he has enough money to buy **two** plane tickets next time around, and is taking her with him! Either way, having her new beau whisk her away to a faraway land is the happy ending to the fairy-tale every girl dreams of.

Whatever the urge is whether biological, cultural, curiosity, or just plain greediness, that motivates a person to travel to new and exotic places; it really doesn't matter. Successful people *want* to explore new places. Even those who work their asses off and value their alone time in their own space still mark those fun getaways down in their personal planners and work calendars, and count down the days until they come face-to-face with the dickwad airport security officer again. It's ironic how most people work their ass off during the sunny hours of each and every day (Monday through Friday); just to earn the money needed in order to spend 7-10 days lying out in the summer sun, in a tropical location with frozen margaritas. They spend every day living towards that vacation, and when it's all said and done, they start all over again, planning and earning money to give them the next break from reality. Whatever yours or your woman's motivation may be, here's a chance to motivate **her** to want to be with you long term…or at least throughout the end of three dates. Let her know you travel on a regular basis, and let her know there's *always* room for her!!

The media projects that in order to truly be a rich, successful, happy person one must make enough money to be able to travel the world in a five-star fashion. The yearning to earn this ultimate lifestyle drives both women and men to work hard in order to achieve these vacations. These perfect getaways include: Europe, Mexico, Rica and Rico, Hawaii, Alaska, Brazil, Sydney-the list goes on. And if you're that type of man who has never been to the following places, because you don't have enough money, well, it's time to change it, Friend! Traveling is only as expensive as you make it. Now, if you're truly the type of man who hates traveling, let the snoozing dogs lie. Do not tell a woman you don't like to travel. It's a complete turn-off. Make plans! Do it for yourself and your woman will follow! Make a plan for next year's summer or winter and tell her about it. Don't say, "I'm thinking of traveling to…" **Tell** her, "Next summer, I'm booking a trip to…" It's not *necessarily* a lie! You have time to follow through.

As for "Mr. I Plan On Retiring By the Age of Thirty". Go fuck yourself. Your plan's not going to work, and even if it did, it means you're working your ass off now, with no fun and no play. A woman is not interested in dating a man who is unrealistically putting his life on hold so he can play later. Call her when you're sixty, and *actually* retired. Seriously, if you are a saver and are planning on living the life after you retire, she doesn't care. Your retirement is *YEARS* away from this exact moment in time. So, don't try to impress her with the faraway dream of living in *Sun City*! Forget *Sun City*! She wants to be in *Paradise City*! NOW!

As for sailing around the world? Don't bullshit it! Do it! Now, this is about the only "retirement plan" a woman will be interested in hearing. Because it's a lifetime goal, that merits lifelong planning! And it's a dream you and your loved one can work towards together, which will be just as fulfilling to you as a couple as it will be to you as individuals.

It only costs ~$20,000 to sail around the world. This includes: money for boat maintenance, food, clothing, and other random necessities. Why haven't you or your woman done this? Possibly, because you haven't found a mate to share this life-changing experience with! Perhaps, it's too much of a commitment that you just don't feel passionate about. Perhaps, one of you have! And if that's the case, you're definitely going to want to act like you're in AWE of her accomplishments. If you blow it off as if anyone could have done it, she'll feel as though you don't appreciate her accomplishments, and move on. On the other hand, if you're the one who has sailed around the world or traveled to faraway lands, don't act like it's a big deal. Otherwise, she'll think you're full of yourself, because your rich mommy and daddy sent you away to international summer camp when you were younger.

Just Kidding!

What you shouldn't say:

"You're like a bull in a china shop! Just kidding!"

"jk"

What you should say:

"Wow...blonde moment?"

"You're really bad at delivering jokes, I see!"

"Just kidding." This simple saying is a simple sign of weakness. Reasons why one says the term, "just kidding," is subjective, but it is usually stated after submitting a punch to someone's ego. The goal of this idiom is to ensure the wounded that it really wasn't for real. The jk-er didn't really mean it! They were just trying to get a rise out of the jk-ed.

Why the "just kidding" phrase is such a turn-off to a self-confident woman is because they *know* you're just kidding. She's either going to get your sense of tendentious humor or think you're a dick! Either way, she should be able to decipher that you're just pre-poking for fun, and find your obnoxiousness attractive. If you overdo it, that's your fault.

Repeated "just kidding's" can be a bore. If a woman notices that you constantly follow each sarcastic statement with a "just kidding", she's either going to lose interest fast or become bitchy. You might get a feisty enough woman to try to make you acknowledge your bad habit, by throwing an objectionable curveball right back at you! "What did you say, little dick?" She'll wait for your confused stare, and then she'll reply in a sweet, high voice, "Just kidding!"

Any guy who says the initials, "J.K." should be punished. And we're not talking about a person's initials, or Harry's creator. We're talking about text lingo. What, are you 14?!?! The same goes for "lmao" and "lol". We don't care if you are young enough to be considered a part of the text generation. We want an educated man who can speak proper English. We're not lenient on Ebonics, which means we're not going to let short message service (SMS) language slide.

It's not cool to say those things out loud, and it's definitely not going to get you laid.

Stand your ground, men! Say what you mean! A woman who is a klutz knows she just acted like a floundering dumbass. Make a joke! Make her blush! It throws her off her game, creating an awkward moment for her, making her in need of assurance. And who's going to be there to give it to her? YOU! But not by instantaneously taking back your sarcastic insult by saying, "I'm just kidding." You're going to do it with a smile, or look. Perhaps a few minutes later you might compliment her on something else, which will make her lose sight of what an idiot she felt like three minutes ago. As a result from your plan of action, she'll be drawn toward you. Why? Because you just took control over her feelings, and once again-a woman who has control over her life wants a man who takes control over her. It's a feeling of relief that they yearn for.

Finally, if you're with a really confident woman, she'll be looking for a guy to call her out. If she says or does anything that can characterize her to be anything but flawless, she'll want a guy to call her out. Should you be a douche about it? Fuck no! Mind your manners! Always be cocky, but don't be a cock. Don't be afraid to make your low blows, but use a smile or a wink! And if you're hitting too far beneath the belt, you'll know soon. When asking your woman to come hither, if she's well endowed, the phrase, "Come on, Tits Magee!" will definitely get that rise you're searching for, as opposed to yelling at your small-chested companion, "Come along, mosquito-bites." If that's the case, you might as well wave good-bye.

Ending on a solid note, stay away from any low blows about unattractive physicalities. If a woman is insecure about any aspect of her external nature, it's not something she can easily brush off. By using positive words, actions, and by accentuating her high-quality traits-feel free to go ahead and tease away! And please stay away from weight comments. Even if it's obvious to you and the rest of the world that she's a twig, don't be that bombastic asshole and call her "Fatty". At that point, if she excuses herself to go to the bathroom you know what she's doing in there…Now look what you've done!

Vote For Summer

What you shouldn't say:

"Back in high school, I was voted *Most Likely to Succeed.*"

"I'm the *nice* guy."

What you should say:

"Go Giants!"

"I plan on climbing Mount Everest one day."

Just like the most popular kids in high school, in reality, the "bad boys" *always* win. It's not that we don't want to *date* the "nice guy", but these two labels can be a bit ambiguous. To be blunt, if you have been labeled the "nice guy", it's probably because you aren't attractive. Girls are either un-attracted to your physical appearance or your personality. Haven't you ever wondered, "If girls want guys who treat them with respect, why do they always go for the bad ones?" The "bad boys" aren't necessarily bad! They are HOT! Obviously, every girl wants a man who treats her right. But we also want someone who can sweep us off our feet….literally. Why did Fiona choose Shrek over Prince Charming? 1) Prince Charming was a douche. 2) The only other available male characters revealed in the movie were overly excessive verbal animals. Bestiality obviously wasn't her thing! Don't let this happy, fairy-tale ending fool you.

Why are women attracted to a tall, dark haired, dark skinned man who steps off his motorcycle? It's the same reason women were attracted to the strapping young fellow who hopped off his horse hundreds of years ago! It's not because there's something sexy and strong between his legs (although, we hope there is). It's evolution, dear Friends! We want a man who is fresh from a fight. Since the beginning of time, women have always chosen men who could protect them and their offspring. It's animalistic, we know. But we are animals, and we are attracted to muscles for a reason. Not only are we intuitively looking for a rough and tough type of man, we are also searching for a man with top notch genes! It may be unconscious, but we are concerned with our progeny's gene pool. An attractive, smart man will help us create striking, intelligent children. Although the nice, fun-loving guy can give us a good time, we are instinctively more attracted to a man who can make us feel safe, and at the same time weak in the knees. Honestly? We want someone who can make us flow with just one glance. Can you do that? If not, here are some suggestions:

If you are obsessed with a sports team, or ten, tell us! We won't get bored if you want to discuss your favorite pro sports teams. Hopefully, the girl is a fan as well. Just limit your conversation. We want to know what types of sports you are into or play, but if you see our eyes drifting after an hour discussion on Coby's 81 vs Chamberlin's 100, switch subjects. If you've never been on a sports team and the topic comes up in conversation, mention that you love playing a game of touch football with your friends. It's just as good, and gives us the idea that you're an active, playful, fun-loving guy! Make sure you have a favorite sport. Even if you don't watch sports, you need to be knowledgeable of at least one. You don't have to have the stats memorized. Just know a couple players on the team and know the rules of the game. How would you feel if your girl knew more about football than you? It's not sexist if it's true!

Act outdoorsy. If you've never gone camping, skydiving, snowboarding or surfing, be open to the idea. We like men who participate in outside activities. And don't think that your brand new Corvette, which you *drive* outdoors, makes you seem more of a mountain man. It's true-a Corvette is sexier than a Corolla. (Either way, if the stick shift is a good enough size, we'll have a good time!) We aren't necessarily looking for a man who doesn't mind being outside. We want someone who will surprise us with a low-budget date from time to time. Picnics in Central Park are always a winner, but if you want to get extra brownie points, take her on a hike to the old park you used to play at as a kid. Just make sure she's got something to wipe with!!!

Women, like men are attracted to particular characteristics. Some like the rugged type, and others like a clean cut man. If she's dead set on a guy with thick, luscious, layered hair and you have a receding hairline, you may be shit out of luck! Don't get nervous though! Most women aren't attracted to these men and these men only. Muscles may not be her thing! Maybe she prefers a shorter version of Justin Timberlake. Think of Tom Cruise! He's 5'7", and before his Scientology days, any girl would have banged the shit out of him!

My Eyes Are Up Here!

What you shouldn't say:

"You are the most beautiful thing I've ever seen."

"I've never gone out with anyone as pretty as you."

What you should say:

"You're a smartass-you know that?" (With a smile on your face.)

"You have such amazing energy about you!"

Of course a woman loves a compliment. I mean, come on! There are *sooo* many you can feed us; it's interesting which one's you choose to. You need to give us a fair amount of compliments, but it's easy to overdo it. You have to be slick and don't tell us lines that we wouldn't believe ourselves. Be charismatic, and make us believe you are complimenting us because it's the truth; not because it makes us feel better, and because you're trying to entice us into bed.

No matter how intelligent a woman is, when dating another intellectual a veiled competition always takes place. It's not that we are trying to impress you by being wittier. We all know the man likes being smarter than his woman-and if you're lucky, we'll make you think you are. See, this is where the problem sets in. As powerful women, we have struggled our whole lives to escape the stereotypical view of the dumb blonde and bring out our sexiness in a more vigorous scholarly way. We know that men love the flaky women, but face it; you are trying to bang a woman of class here! It's going to take more than telling us how beautiful our eyes are or how soft our skin is to get us to open our legs. Our goal is to sound smart without intimidating you. In order to do so, we have to bring our intelligence down a notch. Although we choose to do this ourselves, it's insulting. We'd appreciate it if you encouraged the stimulating, academic dialect and letting us know through comments and facial expressions that you are impressed and amused with our conversation.

It's important not to focus on our looks throughout the night. If you make a woman feel as though you are only dating her because you are attracted to her, she won't want to give it to you. The second you make us feel as though you're paying too much attention to our outer shell, we start second guessing your intentions. And make sure we don't catch you glancing at our cleavage!! If we find you perusing out tits, it may be an automatic out.

Not only do you have to have the right sayings, but you have to have the right timing. If the girl has a sense of humor and makes you laugh, let her know you're enjoying yourself. Just because you're laughing doesn't mean we have you on the hook yet. (For all we know you might be laughing *at* us.) In general, a woman who is funny knows she is funny. We *also* know it's rare for you to find a comical, entertaining woman. If you play your cards right, maybe you'll be lucky enough to keep her around!

If a girl makes a reference that you aren't familiar with, just ask! Don't chuckle and pretend that you know what she's talking about. A-if you're acting like you know a one-liner she just pulled out from the last re-run of Golden Girls, it could get you into a lot of trouble! B-if you ask what she is referring to, it will make her feel more pop-cultured than you. This will make her feel accomplished. Not to mention she may be rethinking your sexuality if you can discuss last night's episode of *Project Runway* better than she, letting your girl believe she can out do you in a pop-culture *Scene-It* game isn't a bad idea. Even though you may have her beat on one-liners from the *Simpsons*, it's always good to let her feel as though she can one up you on trivia-EVEN IF YOU KNOW IT'S NOT TRUE!

In a nutshell, throughout the night make sure you continuously make her feel smart, sexy and funny. Just don't overdo it! If we feel you are laying it on too thick, we'll inevitably think you're in it for the sex and we may just end things right then and there.

Let's Talk About Sex I

What you shouldn't say:

"Does size really matter?"

"I'm a grower, not a shower."

What you should say:

"Sex is fun."

"I lost my virginity at the age of 17."

"Does size really matter?" SERIOUSLY? Do you think a guy with a big dick is going to be concerned enough to ask a girl within the first three dates if size matters? No! He doesn't give a fuck because it's not an issue for him! If you're going to ask your woman this question, you may as well whip it out, let her laugh for a few minutes, and then see if she sticks around afterwards. Even if after you asked this question, you stated that you're a pretty good size, she wouldn't need a lithograph to tell you're lying. If she did, it would look like a fucking earthquake was going off. Face it, this question is more like a confession, not the next random topic you and your lady should be discussing.

There are many sexual things a man can say to a woman that will make her NOT want to sleep with him. For one, if either one of you makes the dumb-ass mistake of asking how many people you've slept with, and your number is low, *don't* let her know. Another common mistake is when bragging about how good you are during sex or your sexual prowess with a stern face, and follow it with a "just kidding" or an insecure laugh. It will make her think you are adequate at the least. If the age of virginity loss is brought up, if yours is anywhere under the age of 15, or over the age of 18, don't tell her. She'll either think you were raped early on, or think you had *really* bad acne. Here's another tip: if you're in a dry spell, don't let her know. She'll question why. You don't want to make her think that you sleep with a different woman every night, but you don't need to tell her how long it's been. This brings us to the next topic of sexual conversations that you should NOT have with your woman:

119

Strippers and prostitutes-No, no, NO! Most women wouldn't give a damn if it were a bachelor party situation, but just in case, avoid all stripper conversations. And if you've had a prostitute interaction of any kind, DO NOT TELL HER! The only word that will come to her mind is "dirty". Yes. She'll instantly form a picture in her head of your dirty cock. Do you really think she's going to want to put your filthy wang inside of her? It's possibly been inside of a hooker! Ew.

Talking about sex too much is a complete turn-off. First of all, the girl doesn't want to *talk* about it all night. Unless she's a dirty, little fuck-which congratulations if you found one, she's going to want it to happen as if she gave you permission to sweep her off her feet and into your bed. The more you talk about it, the less she'll want it. And if your tone is sweet, as if you want to "make love" to her, you're fucked. Do not romanticize fucking. If a girl is sleeping with you within the first three dates, she doesn't want to "make love". Neither of you are in love with each other. You're fucking because you're attracted to each other, like each other's company and are horny! The only sweet thing you should be insinuating is letting her know *if* she sleeps with you, you'll be calling her again.

Please read on to *Let's Talk About Sex II*.

Let's Talk About Sex II

What you shouldn't say:

"Come on. We're both adults here."

"Let's play numbers!"

What you should say:

"I haven't been in a serious relationship recently, because I just haven't found someone that I want to get serious with."

"I don't want to do anything you don't want to do."

Is it wrong to act like there's a future *just* to get the girl in bed? Depending on how sensitive of a woman she is, yes, perhaps she'll be hurt. And please, be respectful enough to call her the next day. After that, you can slowly cut her off, but don't drop off the face of the Earth. The easiest way to do this is to slowly decrease contact. It might take up to a week to do the fade out, but in the end, it'll be much less heartbreaking than a simple text or "no call, no show". Plus, if you contact her afterwards, you won't seem like such a manwhore.

See, there are many ways a man can leak the fact that they are only dating a woman so they can get laid. Unless she's a broad that is in search of a joygasm, she might not follow you under the covers if she thinks you're going to fuck and run (FR). Things you should avoid: acting like sex is medicine for you. If you give any indication that you are addicted to sex, she'll flee the scene. Most people don't believe in that shit, much less want to be with someone that thinks their constant need to get off is a chronic illness. If you act like being a player or pimp is praiseworthy, she's not going to be interested in your Ice-T-like values. Trying to act like sex is no different than Activision's *Call of Duty*, with the "everyone's doing it" type of attitude, is not going to make your woman want to jump into bed with you either. Acting like sex is no big deal might make her squirm. Most women view sex as a big deal, which is why they have values. You have to pass a test before she jumps into the sack with you. And belittling the act of sex is not going to show her that you respect her decision to bang or not to bang.

Near the end of when you're trying to seal the deal, don't start pulling away early. Mentioning that your work load is about to be kicked up a notch, or that traveling is about to get out of control, is going to make her automatically back away. If this girl is looking for anything past a one night stand, she's not going to be attracted to a man who is warning her that his schedule is about to be packed. It's also quite obvious you are preparing her for nothing more than a fuck buddy relationship. If she questions your thoughts on relationships, and you respond to one of the following, she'll be hurt, and clam up: 1) I just got out of a long relationship, 2) I'm just looking to have fun, or 3) I'm not looking for anything serious. If she hears any of these, it'll be REALLY easy for her to justify NOT sleeping with you, even if you are hot stuff. It's automatically telling her there is no future, and you really don't even like her that much. You're just in it for some pussy.

Bringing up sex with multiple partners is not recommended. If you've done it, there's no need to brag about it. In her head, it's not even an accomplishment. It's more like a reminiscent of the night you got those two girls drunk out of their minds. Whether you all played Flip Cup, or you just watched them play with the cup, it will probably not turn her on. Furthermore, do not ask her if she's interested in having sex with multiple partners. Orgy-experienced or not, she does not want to have a conversation with you within the first three dates on how many people she's had sex with at one time. And please avoid asking for her thoughts on girl on girl action. If she doesn't go down under, she's not Australian, and she's definitely not a lesbian.

Going back to the number game, there are reasons why this question is one of the worst questions to bring up on a date. You never want a woman to think you don't have a lot of experience, but if she asks you how many girls you've been with, don't answer with, "Honestly? I don't remember." Not only does that mean that you're a womanizer, it means you don't remember if you've used protection. Remember, the goal is that you *want* her to make the decision to sleep with you...

Please read on to *Let's Talk About Sex III*.

Let's Talk About Sex III

What you shouldn't say:

"Here are my car keys….if I can't get you off, you can have it."

"I'm amazing in bed. Just kidding. No, but seriously…I've had more than enough experience….so…."

What you should say:

"I don't think you could handle this."

"There's nothing my cock couldn't do."

You don't want her to think in any way that she is more sexually competent than you. She's not your mother, and she's not your teacher. You're both old enough to be sexually experienced, so unless you make her think otherwise, she *should* think you're sexually experienced. So if the topic of sex pops up, don't let her think you have any insecurities on the matter.

If sex talk starts, be smooth and modest. Don't act like sex is *just* sex, and don't put the pussy on a pedestal either. Behave as if it's an expensive hobby of yours, and you're skillful enough to nail any black diamond that comes your way. And perhaps if this girl is **lucky** enough, you'll let her join you in your climatic expedition. Make her *want* to hop on your ski lift and work your way up to the climax. And here's how:

When talking about sex, if you do it smoothly enough, you'll turn her on. If you bring up the topic and she laughs it off, rolls her eyes or looks shocked, chuckle it off and switch subjects. But if she gives you a deep look and doesn't slam the door shut, feel free to keep the conversation going. Just stick to the following subjects: places and positions. The rest of the communication should be nonverbal.

"Where's the craziest place you've ever done it?" This question can only be followed by great fun, unless you or your girl are lame asses. If your answer to this question is "in bed", or anywhere located inside of a house, lie. Pick a fun place: an amusement park, a movie theatre, on the pitcher's mound on your college campus, Rutgers Gardens, whatever. It'll cause a laugh out of shock, and that little out of the ordinary sexual experience you share will make her sexual curiosity begin to spark.

If the sex convo continues, bring it on. And here's a secret: if she's talking about sex with you, you have her in bed already. So, have fun and take some CliffsNotes. Ask her what her favorite position is. And when the question is reverberated back to you, *DON'T KNOCK THE MISSIONARY POSITION!* Yes, it sounds like the most boring, but it is the sweetest, most passionate, and probably the one position most girls can actually get off from during coitus. Also, don't mention something disgusting, such as the pastrami sandwich, jelly donut, or every jackass' favorite, the dirty sanchez. Bring a piece of furniture into the conversation. That will peak her interest. So whether you're using a fixed chair for the rickshaw or a rocking chair for the slinky, mentioning any crazy-ass position will make the conversation go on, because she'll end up asking, "What the hell is that!?!?!" The stick shift doesn't actually involve a stick shift, but who knows? Perhaps your sexual dialogue will kick your drive home into high gear and your lady will either jump on you or your ride!

1st Base, 2nd Base, 3rd Base, 4th...

What you shouldn't say:

"May I kiss you?"

"You're so beautiful."

What you should say:

Nothing! Just do!

Although the purpose of this book is to improve your chances of getting laid through conversation, it is imperative that you don't mess up physically as well as verbally. Pay close attention to this topic, and remember when getting physical with your new girl, don't speak! Dirty pillow talk can come later. Keep in mind, these nutshell directions are just an outline, but will definitely help guide you to seal the deal.

First comes first, and what I mean by this is find out if she is interested in you! It may sound simple, but here are some helpful hints and instructions:

On the first date, pay close attention to detail. Don't measure how much we want you by how nice and open we are. We may be labeling you as a new best friend in our heads. An easy way to find out if we want you is to notice if we touch you. A slightest touch to the hand or a bump while walking next to you does not indicate that we waddle like a penguin. Instead, it reveals that we don't mind the lack of space between us. If you feel her hand rub against yours while walking side-by-side, simply say, "Ok. You can hold my hand if you want to," and grab hers. If her instant reaction is a smile or giggle, you're good! If she stumbles, trying to create an excuse, don't try to bang her just yet.

Check her out before and after she enters the bathroom. Earlier in the date, if she has dark or thick lip gloss on and she doesn't reapply throughout the evening, this is a good sign! We are well aware that you do not want to end up with red or shiny lips by the end of the evening. Another easy sign to tell if we are into you is if our disheveled looks have been redone. If we take the time to reapply our make-up and fix our hair in the bathroom, this is a good sign. We obviously want to look good for you! If you were someone we weren't interested in making out with, you wouldn't be worth the effort.

Don't say a cheesy line or compliment how beautiful we look before you go in for a kiss. We know you think we're hot. If you didn't you wouldn't be leaning in for a kiss! You don't have to coax us to kiss you back if we're into you; and if we aren't, we won't be returning the kiss.

If you notice that she is having a great time and you feel as though she is looking for a kiss, lock eye contact and go in for the kill. Don't ask! Don't apologize! Asking and the words, "I'm sorry," are both a sign of weakness. We don't want to have to give you permission to get to first base. We want you to take us! Make it passionate, yet demanding at the same time. If you want something, take it! That determination turns us on. Starting off with a slight open-mouth kiss, which becomes stronger, is good. When making it a deeper kiss, slide your hand from her neck to the ear area. It also helps to push her up against a car or wall. Don't be too forceful, but once we feel your domination, our bodies start to prepare for more intimacy. Sweep us off our feet and don't be messy! A sloppy kiss makes us think you're going to be sloppy in bed. What turns a woman on is a man who knows what he's doing in the bedroom. Your kiss is an indication of how you function in the bedroom. So, show us that you know what you're doing, and if you don't….act like it!

Here is a little hint: If the girl pushes herself on top of you it's a pass to second base. This thrust shows that we are getting turned on. We aren't in high school anymore and second base is no big deal. Come in from the side though. Don't act like you're trying to read Braille. The truth is, we love to have our breasts caressed, and appreciate you when you give us a good chest massage.

As for the second and third date, if you've had a couple of make out sessions, things are going well. Try to take a look at her car after she arrives to your dates. If her rear-view mirror is facing the driver's seat, she took the time to take one last look at her hair and face. We always seem to forget to turn it back until we check our mirrors when driving home.

The key to your make out sessions is no pressure. Unless she is the one reaching down your pants, don't expect you're going further. Just because you got to second base last night doesn't mean you're getting a hand job tonight. The truth is women hate hand jobs! By now, we have mastered the art of the blow job. We don't feel like licking our hands or spitting on your dick in order to decrease friction. A hand job takes twice as long as a blow job and we don't want to waste our time acting like we're freshmen in high school again. We know what you want, and when we are ready, we will give it to you. And I promise if a girl is willing to give you a blow job, she's willing to sleep with you. At this point in her sexual career – she's already thought about it, made the decision, and is waiting for you to pull out a condom. (By the way, keep a condom on you at all times. Be prepared! Just don't let her see it ahead of time. If she sees it stuffed in your wallet, she'll think you're expecting it. If it magically pops out at the right moment, she'll be thankful.)

The last set of instructions is to create a sexual setting at the end of the date. Invite her upstairs to your place, or ask if you can meet her cat upstairs. Any excuse will do, *just not the bathroom! She doesn't want to hear about that.* Plus, while you're in there cleaning up, it gives us time to double think the situation and we'll dry up like the Sahara. You'll need the *Exxon Valdez* to lube us back up. If the make out session lasts longer than ten minutes, your chances are excellent! She's waiting for you to make the move! Now stop rubbing her tits and rub something that counts!!!

Epilogue

Fare-thee-well on your journey, horny men! And heed this advice in stride. As for feeling guilty that you are trying to trick women into sleeping with you by playing with an advantage, fear not! These women have their own brains and they make their own decisions. They are mature, successful women and know the consequences of sleeping or not sleeping with a man. As for all *you* know, you may be accompanying a Lipstick feminist into your bedroom, and if that is the case-good for you! You've beat her at her own game!

Women should not be viewed professionally, domestically, socially or sexually as inferior, innocent beings. In today's world, they are given the right to be treated as equals; therefore, they have the responsibility and obligation to act like equals. There are no excuses, and if they are making the decision to sleep with you sooner rather than later it's because they made that choice. They chose to have sex, despite being labeled as slutty, or giving up power. Why? Because they, are sexual beings too!

So, stop worrying your little brains that someone's going to get hurt. The women this book will help lure onto your penis are not giving up all of their power. They have plenty to spare. Make her think there's a future, whether you believe it or not. It's like playing "house". Women are just as much liars, and they're cunning too. And who knows? True fondness is known to grow. Only in time....only in time....